ITALY
the beautiful

vmb
PUBLISHERS

ITALY
the beautiful

The Beautiful Sea

Photos by *Marcello Bertinetti - Giulio Veggi*

Editorial Director: *Valeria Manferto De Fabianis*

The Beautiful Mountain

Photos by *Marcello Bertinetti - Luciano Ramires - Giulio Veggi*

Graphic Layout *Patrizia Balocco Lovisetti*

9

Preface

There is no doubt that Italy has something truly special about it. Everyone knows as much, everyone says as much, to such an extent that the compliment has become an axiom, a cliché, even. Yet if we take a closer look, it is not easy to say what exactly makes this peninsula so different from an infinite number of other places in the world. Different answers have been given over the centuries by the artists and poets who have lavished their compliments in an attempt to capture the elusive quality of "beauty" that resides in this unusually-shaped land. If one thinks of Virgil or Carducci, for example, it is an indefinable character that permeates the air, earth and water, thus evading pure and simple natural beauty. So it could be described as the longevity of the myth which, especially in regions such as Umbria and Sicily, does indeed still seem to waft through the valleys and along the coastline. There are also those who say that just one glance is all it takes to fall in love with Italy. This love at first sight is in fact so easy that it has been somewhat of a curse for the peninsula, which over the millennia has attracted a relentless flow of armies from every corner of Asia, Arabia and Africa.

Of course, there is a flip side to this gleaming coin: Italy has also been defined as a mere "geographical expression." However unfortunate it may be, this was more of a political than an aesthetic "expression;" but it is worth dwelling for a moment on the exceptional qualities that must be possessed by such a small, insignificant land, which is nonetheless capable of providing beauty for entire populations, from the Alps to the narrow ridge of the Apennines, from the larger islands to the tiniest crag standing in its seas. Perhaps one reason for Italy's undefinable charm is precisely its small size: the peninula never disarms one with infinite, overwhelming landscapes. Instead, it is reassuring how it is so clearly defined by natural boundaries that are among the most recognizable in the world. It has neither oceans of mountains nor plains so vast that they become oppressive; neither does it have endless rivers or cities so immense as to eliminate nature for hundreds of square miles all around. Yet nor is it lacking in any of those things: it has some of the highest mountains in Europe; its cities, large and small, are gems in their own right; its one, large plain boasts record productivity. In Italy, everything is contained on a small scale and thus appears more precious, like a jewel in a treasure chest. Each of its natural or artificial masterpieces of beauty (from the alpine lakes to the ancient villages that all over the country cling to the coastlines or the sides of mountains) is easy to reach, as though it were a treasure trove to enjoy gradually, piece by piece. In a certain sense, Italy can be "possessed."

2-3 Despite progress in science and technology, humanity is still powerless when faced with the primordial force of a stormy sea.

4-5 The Maddalena Archipelago is one of the most picturesque spots of the Italian coast. It still has crystal-clear waters and a dense mediterranean maquis. The island of Budelli can be made out on the left of the picture, while Razzoli is on the right.

6-7 A stormy sky hangs above the island of Capraia and the fortress of San Giorgio, which overlooks the town.

11 In the evening calm, U Dragùn (the Big Dragon) - the legendary vessel that takes part in the traditional annual torchlight procession held on 29th August - rests on the stretch of water before Camogli.

Preface

So we have an Italy that is desirable, so inviting that peoples who have arrived from all over the world have been inspired to call it their "homeland;" but there is also an Italy that is best appreciated for its contrasts, and not for its promises of harmony. In fact, this vast range of beauties is contained and defined by two completely opposite extremes which are, however, so close that they blend into each other.

The mountains and the sea, the protagonists of the pages that follow, are the most constant presence in the peninsula's landscape. They define it entirely and simultaneously, giving it an appearance of togetherness and accessibility. It is impossible to tire of such a varied, complete landscape, or feel distant or excluded from it. The dramatic views of certain alpine faces in no way diminish the tranquil beauty of Italian panoramas: having arrived on the western Alps, even a warrior as down to earth as Hannibal was moved at the sight of the great irrigated plain that was later to be named "Padana." It is almost a play on words, from the Dolomites you see the sea, from the sea you see the Dolomites; it is an endless mirroring of images that have no comparison elsewhere in the world, from the most striking peak to the calmest plain.

However, most of Italy expresses itself through clay, limestone, olive trees and cypresses, offering proportionally the greatest number of beautiful sights. The peninsula meets its three seas along an endless coastline that runs for 4650 miles (7500 km) through the very heart of the Mediterranean; with it, it shows another of its most interesting characteristics, and even one of its fortunes: its centrality. Stretched between two seas that are a maximum of 185 miles (300 km) from each other, the Apenine range slices through one of the richest basins on the planet.

Therefore, as a natural consequence, it gathers every influence coming from the west, from the east and the south, climactic and cultural influxes that settle on a land that seems never to tire of giving and receiving. This brings us to a last, important attraction of the so-called Bel Paese: nature has made it so welcoming that it lies in the most crucial, accessible part of Europe, along its central axis.

Between land and sea, then, Italy can offer itself to reality as well as to dreams. The peninsula is suspended between a myth that is constantly renewed, and physical and human geography that never ceases to amaze; it sets out its brightness from the glaciers to the waves of the sea, reflecting it in an infinite cycle that manages to inspire poets and calm warriors: two elements that each of us can find in ourselves.

13 The Pale di San Martino are some of the loveliest Dolomites in Trent and overlook San Martino di Castrozza.

14-15 The blinding whiteness of the glacier accompanies the trek up to the Capanna Margherita, which was refurbished in 1980. Every year the refuge is reached by some two thousand people from all around the world.

16-17 An aerial view of the Aosta valley peaks in all their splendor; Monte Bianco can be seen in the background.

18-19 The peaks of the Dolomites of Brenta bathed in the early morning sunlight.

The Beautiful Sea

20 and 21 *With different shapes and decorations in each region, boats have always been the most solid bond between people and the sea.*

Introduction by
Piero Ottone

The Italians and the sea: it's a good theme. But it's a misleading theme, because the Italians do not have a steady relationship with the sea; they do not always love it, or they do not love it enough, unlike other peoples such as the Phoenicians, the Vikings or the English, who really can be defined as seafaring peoples. For long periods of their history, the Italians have withdrawn from the sea. Why?

Nobody can claim that they have stayed firmly planted on dry land for a number of centuries only because they were attracted by fertile, hospitable plains. The peninsula's terrain, except for the Po valley and a few other areas scattered around, is mountainous and harsh. For a long time, the inhabitants of the regions that lie south of the Gothic Line lived like island people, because communications with the continent, over the Apennines, were precarious. Yet, in the first part of its history, ancient Rome was a land power,

the Prussia of ancient times, and only when it took on Carthage, the equivalent of England at the time, it had no choice but to become seafaring.

It is true that, having won Carthage, Rome acquired the characteristics of a global power, as strong at sea as it was on land, and some of its generals were also fine admirals. Well-trained fleets quickly moved armies from one end of the Mediterranean to the other, they fought and wiped out pirates, challenged and crippled their enemies; and meanwhile, countless cargo ships, slow and bulging, transported wheat, fruit, amphorae of oil and wine from Africa or Spain to Italy. Yet the empire never took on a seafaring identity. The armed legions, rather than the ships, remained the symbol of Imperial Rome.

Once the empire had fallen, the Italians forgot about the sea and stopped sailing. This desertion lasted until the birth of the

Communes and the seafaring Republics. However, after that splendid period of Italy's history, there was another widespread withdrawal to dry land. Once again, the Italians shut themselves into cities protected by walls, in villages that took refuge in the mountains; the Genoese and Venetians continued to sail as it was their trade, but by now it was in a humble way, lacking in glory. The unification of Italy was also carried out on dry land, and was undertaken by infantries and mounted squadrons rather than admirals and sailors. Garibaldi's slow crossing from Quarto to Sicily on an old steamer was one of the few episodes of the Risorgimento that was connected to the sea, and was not particularly daring or memorable. The best known sea event, that which immediately springs to mind, is a defeat, the battle of Lissa. That defeat, unfortunately, was not the last. The world wars of the twentieth century saw heroic feats by courageous men, episodes of self-denial and sacrifice, the motor torpedo boats, assault crafts, the "pigs" of Alexandria and Gibraltar; but the fleet as a whole met with serious setbacks. This was not only due to the inferiority of its vessels, or to the lack of modern instruments such as radar, but also due to a mistrustful attitude toward the sea, toward seafaring men; so much so that in the theater of operations the unit commander was not expected to do what he thought was right, was not supposed to make spontaneous decisions, but was expected to act according to the orders issued from Rome.

Could a less seafaring mentality possibly exist? Is there a more glaring way to ignore the law of the sea, by which on board, after God, only the captain counts? (Of course, the English left their captains free to make their own decisions as soon as the ships left the port. One evening Admiral Cunningham, in command of the Mediterranean fleet, was unsure whether to continue westward with his squadron, or return to Alexandria. He looked at his watch: "It's lunch time," he said. "We'll decide later." He had lunch; then he decided to continue, and won a battle, at Matapan, which made history.)

Well? Well, the balance would be rather negative, if Italy too did not have its glorious years, the splendid years of the Republics. Five golden centuries, during which the Italians – not all of them, admittedly, but many of them – the Italians of Venice and Genoa, of Pisa and Amalfi, of other cities and other regions from Liguria to Sicily and to Dalmatia (which was also part of Italy), ventured over the seas with agility, nonchalance, with incredible courage, in short, with all the enviable qualities of seafaring peoples.

Italy's seafaring season, when it came, was not just any season. Apart from the fact that it lasted several centuries, it was so overwhelming as to overcome all comparison. Let us now recall Italy's best moments, having remembered her sadder times. Each spring, swarms of the Republics' sailing ships migrated toward the East, loaded with goods carefully watched over by the merchants; they were always on board and, as well as being businessmen, they were also capable of sword fighting and knew a great deal about sailing. The Greek islands of the Ionian and the Aegean, Rhodes and Crete, as far as distant Cyprus, and the Turkish coastlines here covered in prosperous, noisy cities with splendid colors and strong smells, and had Genoese, Venetian emporiums – Italian emporiums, warehouses, bazaars where Italian dialects were spoken.

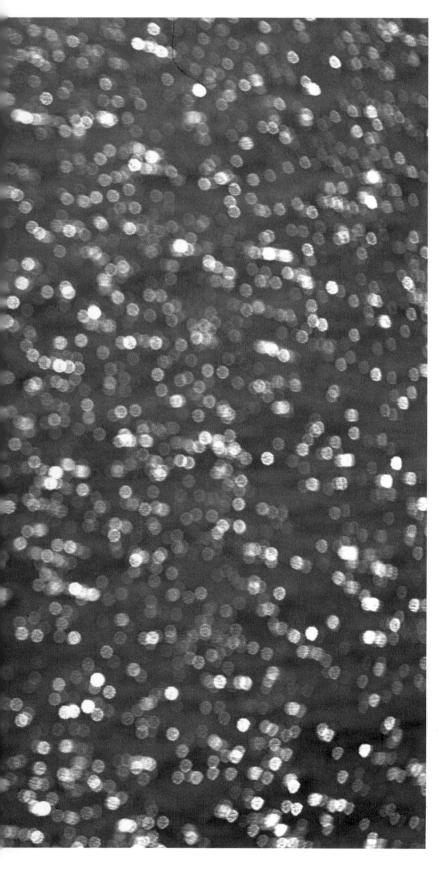

22-23 The infinite expanse of the sea and the absolute freedom of the seagull's flight capture the deepest significance of this particular aspect of nature.

That was not all. Audacious sailing ships pushed across the Dardanelles, beyond the Bosporus, on the Black Sea, as far as Odessa and the Crimea. Others steered toward the Holy Land, to establish a connection with the caravans from India and China. And these adventurous journeys were repeated each year, in ever greater numbers, with ever greater profits. Unless, of course, other expeditions were taking place, of a warlike nature. Suleiman the Magnificent's vast, threatening fleets sailed westward, to strike the Peloponnese or Malta, Tunisia or Sicily, and they had to be fought back.

Warriors' journeys, merchants' journeys: each summer episodes from the same human comedy were played out, alternately, sometimes to the advantage of the Muslims, sometimes of the Christians; this continued until the Battle of Lepanto, which struck a fatal blow to the Turkish power. At Lepanto, alongside Don John of Austria there was an Italian, a Doria from Genoa.

No less important, although less famous in terms of folklore, was trading toward the west, with France and Spain and beyond. A Genoese fleet commanded by Andrea Doria was at the service of the Spanish; Charles V and Philip II of Spain greatly esteemed, and often used, Italian sailors. Beyond Gibraltar the sailing ships that flew the flags of Italy's republics ventured onto the ocean, sailing up the coat of Europe as far as Lisbon, Brittany, Flanders and England; or sailing on the open sea.

The era of great discoveries was to a considerable extent an Italian era. Christopher Columbus immediately comes to mind; but Columbus, with all due respect for his great feats, was one of many. The civilization that was flourishing in those centuries in Western Europe was an adventurous one; men, animated by a conquering spirit, continuously sought out new frontiers. The Italians were among the protagonists of those undertakings, and they had a lot to teach the Catalans or the Portuguese on the art of navigation.

In 1337 Francesco Petrarch wrote in a letter that "...of Brittany, of Ireland and of all the Orkneys in the north of the western Ocean, and the Fortunate Islands in the south of the same, whether through experience, whether by word of mouth of the travellers who pass through there daily, we hear not much less than we hear about Italy and France;" and in 1346 he noted that in the Fortunate Islands "in memory of our fathers a Genoese war fleet was approaching." These were the Canary Islands; it is also likely that the Azores, Porto Santo and Madeira were also reached by the Italians before the Portuguese.

There were five dark centuries in the history of Italy's relationship with the sea; but there were also some golden centuries. Indeed, the golden period was that which coincided with freedom. Only free peoples, masters of their own destiny, go seafaring; and not just because the bonds of political subjection can materially make it impossible to put together fleets and set sail for faraway shores. It is also because the adventure of the sea requires a certain kind of attitude of the spirit, which is in fact the spirit of freedom, of courage, of pride. People do not navigate when they are lacking in faith and mortified; they navigate when they have faith in life, and faith in themselves.

So it happens that for the Italians, the centuries of political and commercial glory, the centuries of the Communes and the Republics, were also the centuries of the closest relationship with the sea. From the 17th century on, when foreign domination began, when the peninsula became a conquered territory and the Republics themselves, while remaining free, depended more or less directly on foreign potentates, the relationship with the sea was interrupted and seafaring traditions dried up. It is true that after the discovery of America, the history of navigation moved from the Mediterranean to the oceans; but it wasn't a fear of the ocean that stopped Italian sailors, who had been the first to plow through it. It

was national discouragement that made them become so attached to the land because, as the poet says, only a free man loves the sea.

Now Italians are free, more or less; Italy has been an independent state for over a century, with the aspiration to stand alongside the richer and stronger states of the western world. So are the Italians rediscovering the sea? Are they rediscovering ancient traditions, from the years when they built solid, swift ships, slightly better than the others', and discovered new routes and attempted new undertakings?

Let us try to provide a sensible, rather than rhetorical, answer. Even in modern times, although new forms of transport have been discovered, although nowadays we are more likely to travel by plane, train or car than by ship, we continue to travel the seas for military objectives, for commerce, for fishing and for sport. In each

24 Although the Mediterranean is having to face serious problems caused by pollution, it still has parts that are practically uncontaminated.

25 A violent wave crashes onto the coastal path at Manarola.

of these activities Italy has the potential to be successful: it has a good navy, supported by an excellent Academy in Livorno. It has shipping companies and sailors in various cities by the sea, from Genoa to Naples, from Palermo to Trieste; the fishing boats fish in the Adriatic, along North Africa, in the Atlantic, and Italy has a certain amount of success in the sports world too, which s destined to become increasingly important.

However, what is still lagging behind is the seafaring mentality. It is difficult to explain the behavior and mentality of a nation that lives in tune with the sea and with its demands; perhaps a few examples could be useful here. It is thanks to the seafaring mentality that in England a voluntary service for sea rescue has traditionally existed for so long: special unsinkable and self-righting vessels are distributed along the coast, suitable for tackling storms; and when somebody is in danger, whether it is a fishing boat, a

26-27 *With a technique similar to that used on* tonnara *boats, fisherman in Camogli lower their nets into the sea.*

28-29 *La Maddalena is the principal island of the omonymous Archipelago, just off the northeast coast of Sardinia.*

30-31 *The calm tranquillity before sunset brings a day of fishing to a close. This picture shows the stretch of sea in front of Praia, on the Amalfi Coast.*

yacht or a ship, the volunteers come to their assistance, day or night, launch the lifeboat, whatever wind or sea conditions there may be, and off they go. In Italy, not even the harbor master's offices have vessels suitable for stormy weather, and should an emergency arise, the port authorities grab the most suitable boat out of those moored in the harbor, and do their best with it.

In England, anyone who wants to set sail on a sporting boat either buys or rents one and leaves: it's that simple. In Italy, they first have to buy a handbook to see how many legal regulations they have to follow. They need a licence, with a tax disc that has to be bought each year; they have to be qualified to use VHF equipment; they need a lifejacket; a rope of a certain length to tie up the lifebuoy; a foghorn; a first aid kit; a bugle, of the standardized variety of course … the list is endless. Does not the very fact that it exists, as the result of grotesque elucubrations of sedentary civil servants in the rooms of some ministry, reveal the most utter lack of trust in those who go sailing? Does it not prove that the State assumes that Italians are all shepherds and have never set eyes on a boat?

Let us continue. An example of a seafaring mentality is a 30 ft (9 m) yacht that arrives in Corsica with paint peeling off its hull, with its sails frayed on the after-edge, and dad, mum and a couple of kids between five and ten years old on deck. These are Bretons or Provençals, probably, and will have faced and experienced, in their microcosm, and adventure which is not entirely unlike, although on a different scale, the great historical navigation undertakings, the discoveries of other centuries. I am not saying that the Italians are not able to do the same, but if that little 30 ft (9 m) boat, with its peeling hull, is the symbol of sporting France, the Italian symbol would be a 66 ft (20 m) cabined powerboat, an "iron."

Weather forecasts are mainly useful to those who are going sailing (and to those who fly, as well: but aviators receive the forecasts directly at the airport, before setting off). However, in Italy, they are provided by the Air Force's meteorological service, not by the Navy; therefore, by officials who institutionally do not have the seafaring mentality. What do 70 knots of wind matter to someone who's flying? For its part, RAI (Italy's national broadcasting service) broadcasts the reports as and when, at uncertain times, at the end of the radio news which lasts varying lengths of time, after having narrated the exploits of De Mita and the prowess of A.C. Milan. It is all too evident that they broadcast the weather reports reluctantly. In France, the weather forecasts are authentically marine; in England the BBC interrupts the program for a storm warning. When has a program ever been interrupted in Italy? Just as well, really, because Italian weather forecasts bear little relation to actual facts.

In Italy, complicated, contorted laws hamper trade navigation and the running of harbors, with absurd obligations; and laws do not come out of nowhere, rather they reveal a mentality that is not in tune with the sea. Luckily, not all Italians are as scarcely inclined to seafaring as the representatives of the ruling class; luckily, the seafaring spirit exists, and is making progress. Italy is like an old giant who, after a long period asleep, is regaining consciousness and little by little remembering what he used to do before he fell into his slumber. The memories are intoxicating and conjure up illustrious names – Vivaldi and Cabot, Christopher Columbus and Andrea Doria; traces of Italy's seafaring past can be found along its coasts, in villages and seaside cities, Genoa and Camogli, Naples and Amalfi, Venice and Trieste and Monfalcone and Ragusa. Just as other such traces exist in Greece and in Turkey, on Crete and Cyprus, in the Canaries and on Madeira, in the Caribbean…. Little by little, the giant is becoming enthusiastic, and is returning to the sea.

But he has to contend with resistance, mistrust, hostility, in a country which, after centuries of darkness, is finding it hard to rediscover its relationship with the sea.

32 top Along the coast of Sardinia, the transparency of the water and the various shades of the rocks beneath it create unusual color contrasts.

32 bottom The Promontorio di Portofino National Park stretches along the sea for almost 2 miles (3 km), between the Golfo Paradiso and the Golfo di Tigullio.

33 The white volcanic cliffs of the Pontine Islands stand out in sharp contrast against the sky.

Of coasts and islands

A seascape cannot be taken in at first glance. It takes time and several appraisals before one can grasp its differences and constants.

The great,
wild island

34   Its abundant wild-growing vegetation makes the area around Punta Falcone the ideal habitat for numerous bird species.

35   The sea in the Stintino area is tinged with extraordinary shades of color, varying from turquoise to deep blue.

36-37   The gloomy atmosphere of a storm bears down on Capo San Marco, the furthest point of the Sinis peninsula.

38 and 38-39   A violent stormy sea thrashes the coasts of the Sinis peninsula.

The dunes of Piscinas, near Ingurtosu on the western coast of Sardinia, create a natural landscape that is unusual for the Italian coast: an endless series of sandy dips come one after the other toward the sea. Moved by the wind, the extremely fine sand shifts into the plants, almost imitating the movement of the waves that ripple the blue surface beyond.

Situated in the northern area of Sardinia, Capo Testa is one of the island's most remarkable areas in terms of natural interest. Saved from the seasonal influx of tourists, the sea here has maintained an extraordinary transparency, in which the rocks reflect their vast variety of shapes and colors.

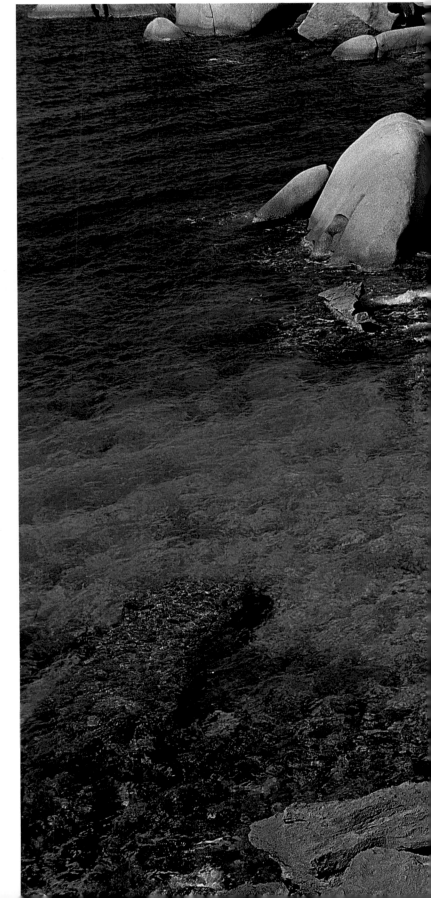

The Azure Archipelago

44 and 44-45 As the light and the weather conditions change, so does the appearance of the sea and the coasts of the Maddalena Arcipelago.

46-47 The church of the Madonnetta dei pescatori ("Little Virgin of the Fishermen") was built on the Isola della Maddalena, overlooking the sea.

48-49 Panoramic view of the north coast of the Isola della Maddalena.

The Maddalena Arcipelago occupies an overall area of 17 sq. miles (43 sq. km). It consists of seven main islands: La Maddalena, Caprera and Santo Stefano to the south-east, Spargi, Budelli, Santa Maria and Razzoli in the north-east.

The Isola della Maddalena is the largest in the archipelago, and is the only one with a town.

50 and 51 The island of Budelli has a surface area of just 1.6 km² and is separated from the islands of Razzoli and Santa Maria by the Passo Chiecco di Morto. It has less than 6.2 miles (10 km) of coast-lines, but among its beaches it boasts the famous Spiaggia Rosa ("Pink Beach") which is undoubtedly one of the most picturesque in the whole of Italy.

The islands of the
Tuscan Archipelago

52-53 *The island of Giannutri, the southernmost island in the Tuscan Archipelago, is completely private except for 16-ft (5-m) strip of state-owned land at the water's edge. It is linked to Porto Santo Stefano by a regular hydrofoil service.*

53 *Pianosa, which is of lime-stone-tufa origin, has an average altitude of 66ft (20 m). It appears as a strip of flat land which is wild and has little greenery. It houses a penal complex and is not open to tourists.*

54-55 Seen from above, the island of Montecristo looks like a huge block of granite. It was declared a nature reserve in 1971 and the only buildings on it are the houses of the guards and the forest rangers, and a splendid villa which once belonged to King Victor Emanuel III.

56-57 The island of Elba, which nowadays is a firm favorite with large numbers of tourists, retains clearly visible traces of its rich history.

58-59 With its dense mantle of larches, pines and olive trees, Gorgona is perhaps the most picturesque of the smaller islands in the Tuscan Archipelago. As there is a detention center on the island, it is not freely accessible to the public.

The red cliffs
of Capraia

The recently closed penal colony has meant that the island has been saved from environmental damage; this is why Capraia, which has now been made a Nature Park, is so incredibly wild and unspoilt.

62-63 Capraia's environmental characteristics make it the ideal habitat for numerous species of seabirds, including the rare Audouin's gull.

64-65 The tortuous coastline and rocks reveal the geological process which, through frightening telluric disruptions of volcanic origin, brought the island to the surface.

66 and 67 Scrubland of helichry-
sum and tree spurge interrupt the
reddish color of the trachibasalt
rock at Cala Rossa.

The white
Pontine islands

The archipelago of the Pontine Islands is made up of Ponza, Gavi, Zannone, Palmarola, Santo Stefano and Ventotene. The islands' volcanic origins are clearly visible on the white rocks, which rise out of the sea, creating a remarkable contrast.

70-71 The large cliff at Punta Capo Bianco, situated north of Chiaia di Luna, shows obvious signs of erosion caused by the wind and sea.

72-73 An aerial view of the Isola di Palmarola, which is the northernmost of the Pontine Islands. Of volcanic origin, like the others in the group, it has very jagged and stunningly beautiful coasts, including the Faraglioni di Mezzogiorno and the Cattedrali.

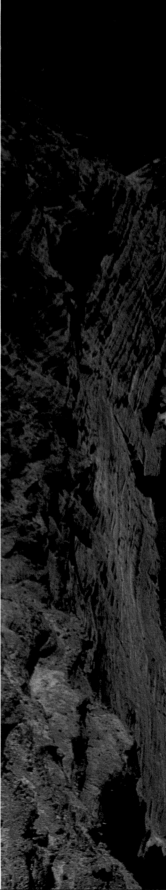

74 Dedicated in ancient times to the god Hephaestus, Vulcano is the farthest south of the Aeolian islands. It has black rocks and beaches with very fine volcanic sand, and has several craters and fumaroles. Its last period of activity was in March 1890.

74-75 Salina's volcanic origins can be clearly seen in the cliff of Pollara.

75 top left Alicudi, which in ancient times was called Ericusa, owes its name to the dense heather shrubs that cloak its harsh slopes in the spring. The western side of the island is deserted, while the east is inhabited and cultivated.

75 top right The small town of Pollara stands at the bottom of what remains of a large, semi-circular crater which was formed about 13,000 years ago in the western part of the Isola di Salina.

*The lighthouse
of the Tyrrhenian Sea*

Stromboli emerges from the abysses of the Tyrrhenian Sea, rising for over 3036 ft (920 m) above sea level. Two hundred metres below its peak, which is known as "Serra Vancura," the currently active crater opens up. The lava flows that run down the Sciara del Fuoco, eventually extinguishing themselves in the seawater, are always a very spectacular sight.

80 The island of Lampedusa, arid and flat, is the southernmost part of Italy and covers around 8 sq. miles (20 sq. km). Its high, sharp coastline rises above brightly colored water which is extraordinarily full of sea life.

81 Linosa's volcanic origins are clearly visible in the conformation of the lavic rocks at Cala Luna, which drop vertically into the sea.

82-83 The lack of freshwater springs and the high temperatures, which easily reach 40°C in summer, make it difficult for vegetation to grow here; it mainly consists of prickly pears and Mediterranean maquis.

84 top Much of the activity of those who live in the towns at the mouth of the River Po takes place on the water.

84 bottom A fishing boat returns to harbor, followed by a crowd of gulls and other seabirds.

85 For fishermen, nets are their main work tool, which is why particular care and attention is given to them.

People at the water's edge

The inhabitants are intrepid seafarers, tireless and proud of their work as fishermen; they are highly skilled sailors, faultless experts on the waves and currents. They have an energetic appearance, like their faces, modeled by the effort of rowing and fishing with nets, and scorched by the salty wind.

Fishermen:

a lifetime for the sea

The life led by seafaring people is certainly neither easy nor comfortable. The satisfaction that they may get from it is not always in proportion to the work, the effort and the sacrifices required of them and imposed on them. Yet a strong bond connects fishermen to their boats and to the end-less expanse that they find themselves covering and comb-ing each day, a complex bond made up of trust and fear, and of intimacy and awe. The sea, everyone knows, cannot be bridled or dominated, but it is important to know it and know how to predict its sudden changes. The following images show some moments from a day spent with a group of fishermen from the Isola della Maddalena.

Once the fishing trip is finished, there is still work to be done: it is necessary to check and repair the nets. They are laid out on the wharf and scrupulously inspected and prepared to face another day at sea. The hands of the fishermen doing this work move surely and quickly, like the hands of a seamstress embroidering cloth.

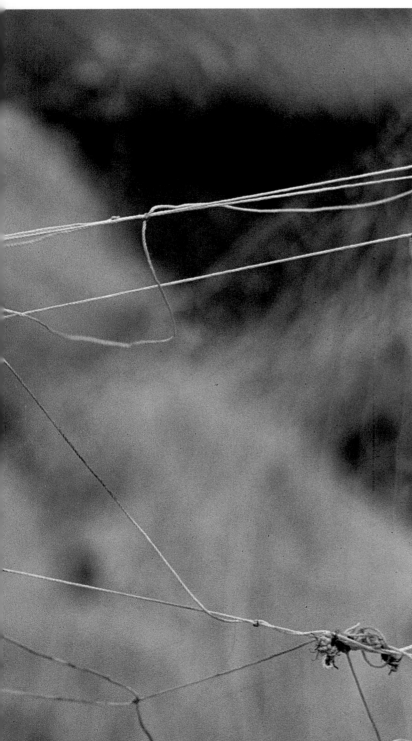

A few decades ago, when *tonnara* (a method for fishing tuna) was still very profitable, hundreds of men flocked to Favignana even from far-off villages and islands for the season of the tuna massacre, which goes from May to June. They abandoned their usual work and for just under a month became *tonnaroti*, and lived through the tiring but exciting experience of tuna fishing. Even today, the nets placed in the sea form a huge, lethal trap in which tuna fish go to die; but while in the past, the season brought in thousands of fish, today only a few hundred are caught. The tradition of the tuna massacre is therefore destined to disappear, or to turn into an annual tourist attraction.

94 Favignana, the main island of the Egadi islands, is the most important center for the tonnara. *The photograph shows the small harbor.*

94-95 The leaden sky accentuates the wild character of the rocky, jagged coast of Punta Bombarda, on the Isola di Marettimo.

95 top A striking portrait of some elderly tonnaroti *on the island of Favignana.*

94

The tonnara's origins date back to ancient times when Sicily was under Arab rule; even today, many of the words in the tonnaroti's language originate from Arabic. The tonnara is governed by rigorous organisation, precise codification and a hierarchical structure that must be strictly respected. The undisputed boss is the rais; in addition to being the expert on the ancient technique, it is his job to study and interpret the "suggestions" given by the sea and the sky.

*Professions
on the sea shore*

Numerous artisanal activities have developed around fishing, whether directly linked or closely connected to it. In small seaside towns, there are still workshops in which the oldest traditions are revived daily through the gestures, the techniques and the materials used.

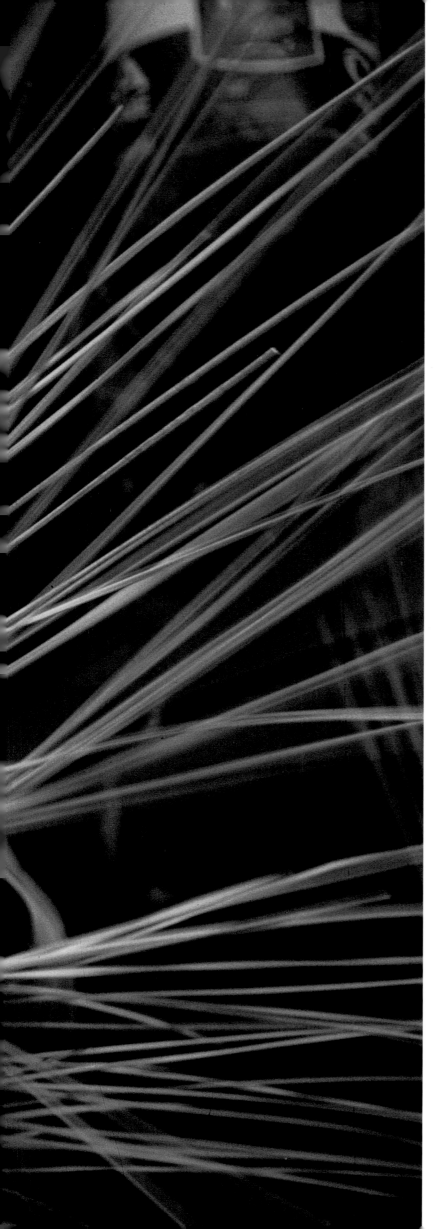

A city by boat

The gondola as it appears now dates back to the 16th century, when the Senate decreed that it should be painted black but it is descended from a very old type of boat, probably already in use before the year 1000.

Even today, it is built entirely according to the same artisan traditions in "squeri," and is the concrete manifestation of a precious, delicate balance between form and the distribution of weight, elegance and efficiency.

More than any other city, Venice lives with water and on water. Every activity, from commerce to transportation, from parties to weddings or funerals, takes place on its canals. Indeed, its charm is inextricably linked to the water, to the wavering reflections of the ancient palazzos, to the colorful boats for transporting goods that blend in without clashing with the elegant, sober line of the gondolas.

110 and 111 Each morning, large numbers of motorboats laden with fruit and vegetables converge toward the Rialto bridge, near the city's largest fruit and vegetable market.

All occasions in the Venetian folklore calendar are in some way related to water. Among them, the most traditional are perhaps the regattas, which began long ago in 1315. Meanwhile, the Vogalunga rowing race was created much more recently, in 1975, responding to the need for large-scale popular events which in towns and cities "on dry land" take the form of group marches or cross-country races. Right from the beginning the Venetians have taken part in the Vogalunga with great enthusiasm.

The Padellata
of Camogli

Without fail every year on the second Sunday in May, the fishermen of Camogli turn into cooks and for a whole day, they dedicate themselves to flouring and frying fish; in the splendid setting of the little harbor, the fish is then given out free of charge to crowds of spectators. The "Padellata" ("Fry-up") was established in 1952, and since then it has taken place each year to growing interest. Indeed, more than 30,000 people, attracted by the originality and fame that this unusual Fish Festival has achieved, flock to the small seaside town.

For the first few years of the Camogli Fish Festival, several frying pans 28 inches (70 cm) in diameter were used, set out along the seafront and the harbor. Then, in order to solve organisational problems, somebody came up with the idea of making the biggest frying pan in the world. the one used today, which is the third generation, measures 13 ft (4 m) in diameter and has a 20-ft (8-m) long handle that acts as a gangplank. It contains 130 gallons (500 litres) of oil and is heated by liquid gas. It is the only one of its kind and is often requested by other towns or villages for their own festivals and events.

120

*Sailing along
the coasts*

The yacht is undoubtedly the best way of directly approaching the sea and nature without violating them and altering their highly delicate equilibrium.

Encounters

126 For people who sail, encounters with sperm whales are always a thrilling moment.

127 Silent and discreet, the yacht makes it possible to get close to a shoal of dolphins plowing through the waters of the Mediterranean.

Amerigo Vespucci

The Italian Navy's training ship, *Amerigo Vespucci*, was built in the naval shipyard at Castellammare di Stabia, to a design by Francesco Rotundi, the Lieutenant-Colonel of the Naval Engineers. Its line is a clear reference to the vessels of the 19th century, with a total length of 333 ft (101 m) and a maximum breadth of 53 ft (16 m). It was launched on 22nd February 1931 and has three masts with square sails, a mainsail aft, a long bowsprit with jibs and stay sails. It is the oldest ship currently in the fleet of the Italian Navy and is undoubtedly the most prestigious, bringing together the deepest meanings of ancient, glorious traditions.

The *Amerigo Vespucci* is used by the pupils of the Livorno Academy and can hold about 500 men. The training period runs from the beginning of spring to the end of summer; in the fall, the *Amerigo Vespucci* goes back to the yard, where it undergoes careful checking and maintenance work. In 1955, to accompany the ship in Livorno, the *Palinuro* joined the ranks of the Italian Navy; it is used by the cadets of the Crew School of the Maddalena.

History on the seabed

It was scuba diving that unveiled the treasures of underwater Italy. Going with mask, flippers and spear gun in hand to make attempts on bream and umbra, along the coasts of the country with the longest history out of all those lapped by the Mediterranean.

Amphorae, terracotta vases, stone or metal anchors lie on the seabed, covered and protected by coral and incrustations. The debris most commonly found along the Italian coastline is of course Roman, especially from after the 4th and 3rd centuries b.C.

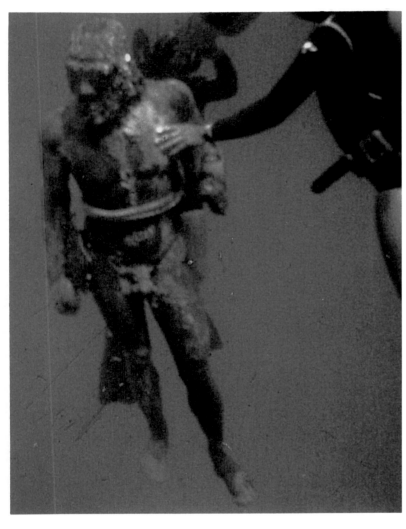

134 This image immortalizes the exciting retrieval of the bronzes of Riace, which are now in the Archaeological Museum of Reggio Calabria.

134-135 Discovery of a Corinthian helmet from the 6th century B.C. on the seabed off the coast of Sicily, near the Greek settlement of Camerina.

136-137 Mounting fixed frames for photographic surveying in the Sea of Miseno.

138 top The houses at Porto Pidocchio on Punta Chiappa go right down to the sea.

138 bottom Located in the heart of the largest town on the island of Capri, the piazzetta is a summer meeting point that is famous the world over.

139 A picturesque image of the town and little harbor of Salina.

Stones and men

Stretched out along the coast, the little houses seem to back up the nature of the headland. In rows, in groups, they hid in the shade of the Mediterranean maquis, almost as though fearful of the sea that is before them.

Sea storm

A violent sea storm crashes onto the fishing village of Camogli, in the Golfo Paradiso. The impetuous power of the squall spares neither the town nor the little harbor, and the waves rise up to completely cover the wharf. People stop, open-mouthed, to admire this fascinating yet dramatic spectacle, well aware that the strength of the sea can overcome the work of humans.

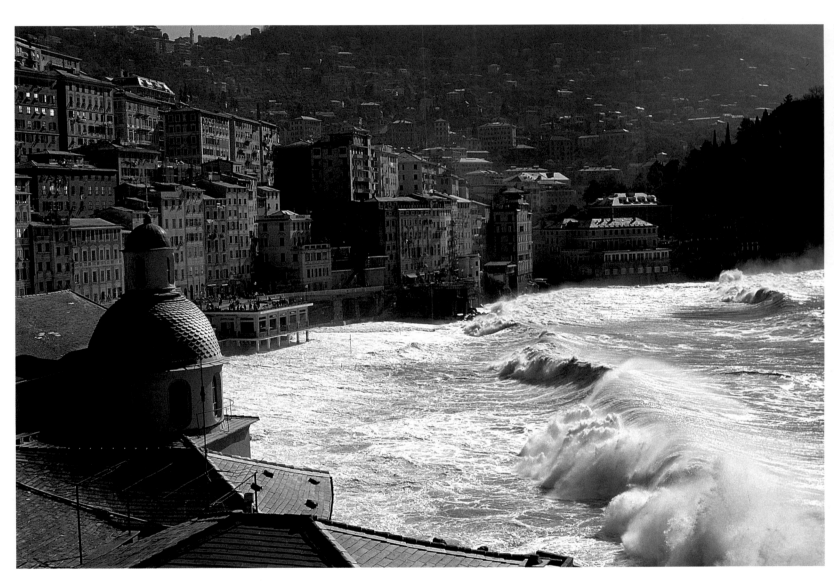

The colors of Portofino

Portofino is world famous for its natural beauty and for the fashionable high life that takes place there. It is a feast for the eyes, with a marvelous contrast of colors ranging from the purplish-blue of the sea to the bright green of the vegetation on the headland and the hill behind it, to the white of the sails and luxury yachts. The façades of the houses, painted in the typical Ligurian colors of yellow, red and pink, give the whole bay a particularly charming look.

The houses in Portofino stand around the little harbor; to make up for a lack of space, they are built upward. The façades are decorated in a sober, elegant style, and colorful bunches of geraniums hang down from balconies and windows. Stunning villas can just be made out, veiled by the greenery of the hills; they mainly date from the 18th century and have been renovated more recently.

Between rock and sea

Monterosso, Vernazza, Corniglia, Manarola and Riomaggiore: in less than 4 miles (6.5 m) of coast, five villages set into the rocks, standing over the sea, surrounded by terraced vineyards that allow excellent local wines to be produced. These are clusters of tall, narrow houses painted warm colors; they have been built in an extremely inaccessible spot where there is not one beach, not one flat area and much less the space to built a carriage road.

156 top View of Riomaggiore at sunset.

156 bottom The faces of the Ligurians are marked by the strength and tenacity of seafaring people.

157 A spectacular view along the coast of the Cinque Terre.

158-159 Perched high on an impervious cliff, Manarola stands firm against the waves of a violent squall.

160-161 The warm awakening of Portovenere rocks boats anchored at Calata Doria as the dawn lights up the parish church and the mighty 12th-century Genoese castle, set on a hill that dominates the Cinque Terre as far as Punta Mesco.

162-163 The light of the sunset adds extra charm to this matchless stretch of the coast of Liguria.

The painted island

Burano is in fact made up of four islands; it is striking due to its small houses painted in gaudy colors: the yellows, greens, reds and blues of the façades are reflected in the water and mix prettily with the strong colors of the fishing boats.

Since the 16th century Burano has been famous for its lace, which is sold all over the world. Walking along its lanes, one often comes across courtyards full of laundry hung out to dry, lace-makers chatting and fishermen roasting fish or repairing their nets.

The pearl of the
Lower Tyrrhenian Sea

172 top A nighttime image of the port of Ponza and the town above it.

172 bottom The whitewashed convex roofs are used to collect rainwater.

173 Ponza's fishing fleet works actively in the Mediterranean. The picture shows a boat for swordfish fishing.

174-175 The island, which is of volcanic origin, consists of very friable lapillus and tufa rocks that have created an endless sequence of bays, little coves, inlets, promontories, cliffs and isolated crags.

Ventotene:
harsh and wild

176 and 177   Halfway between Ponza and Ischia, the small island of Ventotene covers just over 0.62 sq. miles (1 sq. km). It mainly consists of tufaceous rocks, and contains some precious historic remains.

The Amalfi Coast

The Amalfi Coast stretches between the Bay of Naples and the Bay of Salerno: towns with unmistakeable architecture and colors alternate with Saracen towers and the greenery of citrus groves. Stunning views can be had from the coastal road, which runs high up alongside the incredibly clear sea. It is an irrepressible overflowing of scents and typically Mediterranean plants: oregano, rosemary, strawberry trees, honeysuckle, umbrella pines and larches.

178-179 On one of the most beautiful stretches of the Italian coastline, between the cobalt sea and the highly fragrant Mediterranean maquis, stands the town of Positano, with its steep flights of steps that run down to the beach.

180-181 and 181 The main center of Amalfi is concentrated in the bay of the harbor. The houses are built in the regional style of Campania; the colors range from white, which becomes blinding in the daytime, to the soft pastel colors of the houses on the sea. The typical barrel-roofs, built using an ancient technique, not only collect rainwater but also act as insulation.

182 top At the end of a day's work, fishermen from Amalfi return to dry land.

182 bottom The sunset lights up the typical houses of Amalfi, perched on the rocky spurs of the Monti Lattari.

183 The famous rock of the "Madonna and Child" stands sheer above the sea at Furore.

184-185 The golden rays of the sun at dusk reflect off the sea and bathe the coast of Amalfi. This is a landscape that enchants even in winter, with the dark sky, the few white houses below the rocks and just the fishing boats on the water.

186-187 An unusual image of Amalfi, captured during a brief snowfall.

188-189 After the rain, the rainbow makes its appearance; emerging almost magically from the water, it seamlessly blends the blue of the sky with that of the sea.

*A corner
of the Orient*

Situated between the far point of Capo Miseno and the Isola d'Ischia is Procida; lushly green and rich in vegetation, the island has extremely fertile volcanic soil. The jumbled Oriental-style architecture of the small houses, carved partly out of the tufa and embellished with steep stairways and arches, has remained unchanged over the centuries; so has the small harbor of the Corricella, overlooked by the ancient castle which today is used as a prison.

192 As ever, the quay is bustling with activities linked to fishing. Together with agriculture, it is the islanders' main source of income.

193 The little harbor of Corricella is enclosed by the fishermen's houses. Once painted bright colors, they are now relentlessly faded by the sun and the salty air.

194-195 A night time view of Procida: the houses that are typical of this island are reflected in the water at the small harbor of Corricella.

A mosaic of colors

Linosa certainly offers an unusual and picturesque sight: against the dark lavic rock and the deep blue of the sea, the island has a true palette of pastel shades. The houses are painted white, pink and green, and the doorways and windows are bordered by strips of bright color. The custom of painting the houses in this style dates back to more than 150 years ago, when the Bourbons ordered the first colonies to be built on this, the farthest outpost of Italy.

No more than 450 people live on the island of Linosa; they make their living doing the work typically done in Mediterranean seaside towns. For some years now, each summer the usual rhythm of life is disrupted by the arrival of tourists; but at the end of September everything goes back to normal, and the usual tranquillity returns.

The village
on the waves

The old fishing village of Chianalea, the oldest part of Scilla, is built entirely on the sea. The signs of time and the close contact with the sea can be seen clearly on the façades of the old houses; they are lapped by the waves, which can sometimes be violent and unpredictable.

204 In the summer months, the coasts of Italy take on a different appearance, covered in Mediterranean maquis and multicolored blossoms of various flower species.

205 Cormorants are frequent visitors to the Mediterranean Sea.

Beneath the sky and the water

From dawn to dusk, seagulls incessantly trace out their bold, white flights over the coastal ridges of this world of land and water.

The Spiaggia Rosa

The Spiaggia Rosa ("Pink Beach") is a small bay on the south-east of the Isola dei Budelli. It takes its name from the color of the sand, which is made up of a very fine powder of granite, shells and other minuscule marine organisms. It makes a spectacular contrast with the transparent, turquoise water.

Spring encounters

On a clear day in May, while walking in the absolute calm of the Spiaggia Rosa, a truly unique event occurred: an unexpected encounter with an octopus that was swimming just below the surface of the water.

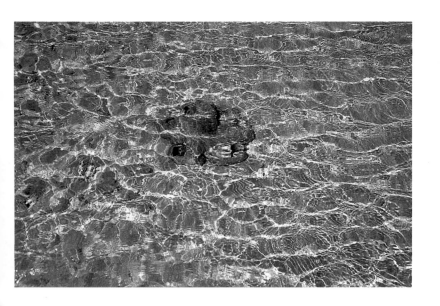

In the silent world
of coral

Colonies of yellow and orange sponge, red coral, sinuous, multicolored soft-corals, rock faces that plunge sheer into the blue, silent shadows that shyly refuse any encounters: in short, this is the most secluded panorama of the Mediterranean. The seabed reveals an incredibly rich, varied landscape, which should dutifully be protected and safeguarded from any further contamination.

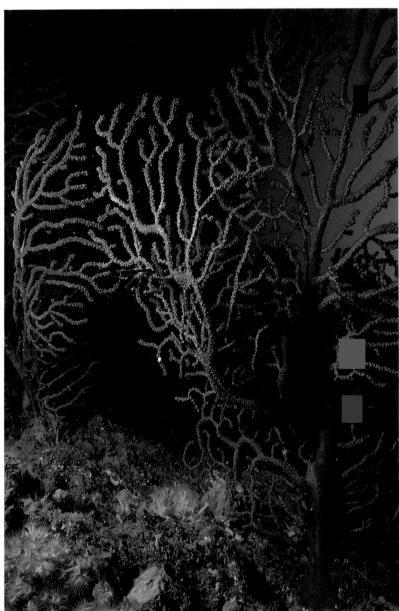

214 Coral and sea-fans cover the rocks on the seabed, in the protected area of the sea around Ustica.

215 A little blenny curiously pokes its head out of its lair.

216-217 A sea-fan creates unique embroidery-like shapes against the background of the sea.

218 Beneath the surface of the sea, nature indulges her whims, creating astonishing new forms of life.

218-219 The scorpion fish is one of the sea-dwellers most commonly found on the bed of the Mediterranean Sea.

219 top The current causes a splendid soft-coral formation to ripple rhythmically.

220-221 *A shoal of amberjacks lights up the seabed with silvery shimmers.*

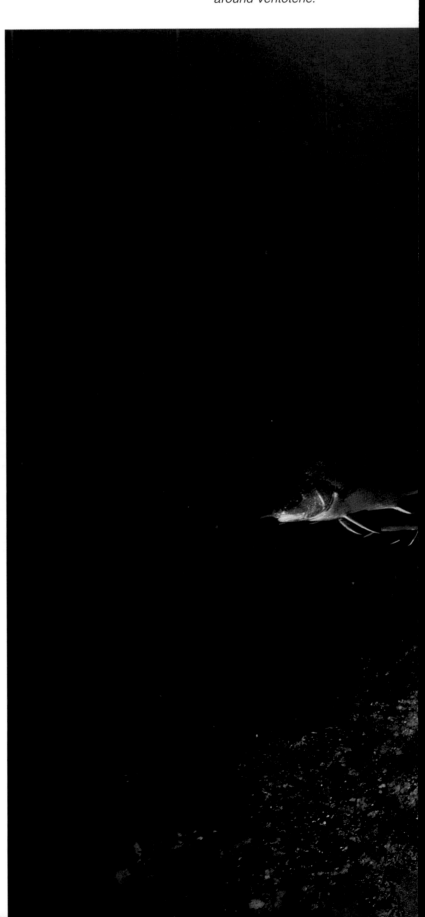

223 top left *The seabed typical of the sea around the island of Lampedusa.*

223 top right *A small shoal of mullet photographed in the sea around Ventotene.*

222 *Both curious and bothered by the light of the electric torches, a congereel comes out of its lair.*

222-223 *A shoal of umbra swims on the rocky seabed of the Tremi- ti Islands.*

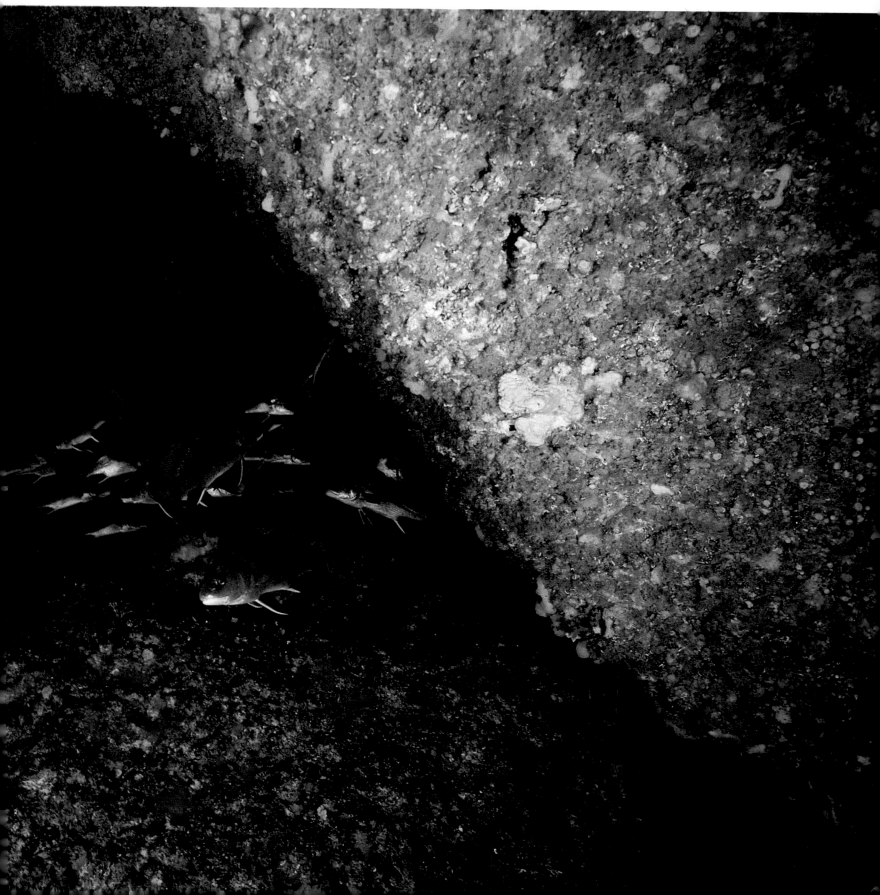

224 A small cuttlefish, frightened by the presence of the diver, takes refuge in the dense clumps of seaweed.

224-225 A group peeps out from behind some rocks.

Flying above the sea

Flying above the sea

The wild nature
of the islands

230 and 231 The island of Caprera has over 28 miles (45 km) of coastline, with a close succession of inlets, headlands, coves, high cliffs sheer over the sea, full of flowers and plants typical of coastal areas.

232-233 A typical example of the lush vegetation that covers the coast between Palau and Capo Testa.

234-235 The coasts of the island of Lampedusa have maintained their natural beauty intact, as they have been saved from the summer invasion of tourists.

The Beautiful Mountain

236 Silhouette of the Monviso lightly veiled in cloud.

237 The rays of the setting sun fall evocatively on the snow-capped peaks of the Aosta Valley.

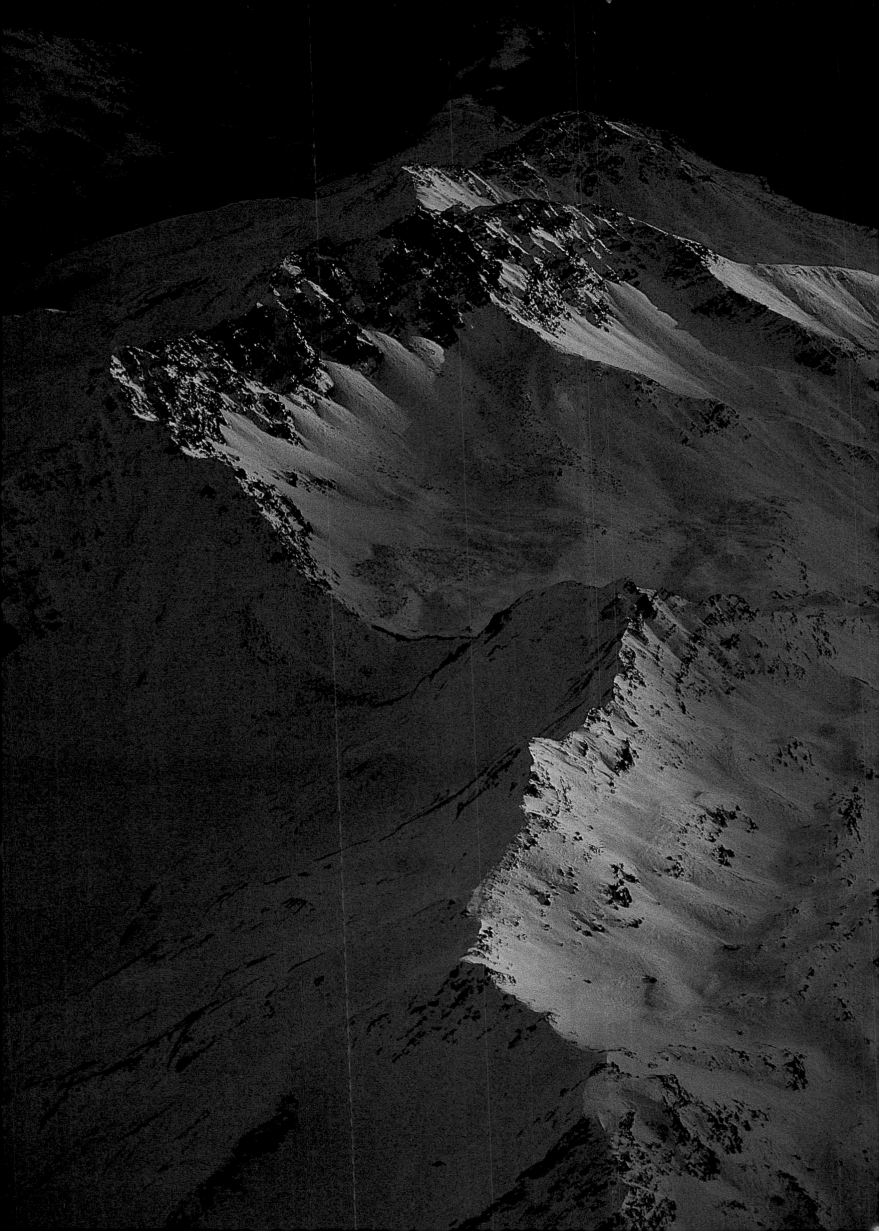

Introduction by
Cosimo Zappelli

I was six years old when, perched on the crossbar of my father's bicycle, I first came near to a mountain. Unconsciously, without knowing why, I approached this infinite and gigantic world with a mixture of amazement and awe, despite hearing the 'grownups' say that men ventured "up there" because of the beauty of the mountains.

"I will lift up my eyes to the hills," wrote the author of the Psalms; yet who know how many others before him had composed similar lines, their eyes searching the mountain peaks for something that would aid both physical survival and spiritual edification. In the Old Testament God is referred to as the "Most High;" Heaven is always situated above the clouds and Hell is always sunk deep in the ground. Apollo and the nine Muses dwelt on Parnassus, and Jupiter and other gods shared a magnificent abode on the highest mountain peak of Greece, Olympus. Over three thousand years ago

Zoroaster descended from a remote mountain in Iran to preach the doctrine of Ormuz; Buddha, the 'Enlightened,' saw the light in Nepal, the land of mountains, and the Hittites worshipped a god of the mountain peak, the lord of storms, thunder and rain.

It was on Mount Tabor, the "high mountain" of the Gospels, where Jesus "led Peter, James and his brother John and was transfigured before their eyes."

All these different populations and cultures have one mysterious factor in common – that of the impenetrable mountain, the seat of the gods and of terrible demons. Since ancient times, what man has attempted to achieve with his knowledge nature has already created through its structures and instilled in his heart, a powerful spell with remarkable contrasting influences, linking past, present and future in unbroken continuity.

If we look at a simple physical map of Italy we can see very clearly how limited the plains are, while a closer examination of the morphology of the land reveals that the entire peninsula and its islands are characterized by great and small mountains and by innumerable and multiform structures known as relief.

The most impressive and most compact mountain range in Italy is the Alps, which stretch like a diaphragm across the entire northern part of the country for a length of approximately 620 miles (1000 km). This is intersected by the Apennines, a mountain range that runs longitudinally like a backbone down the whole length of the peninsula, from north to south, from Liguria to Calabria, also for a length of around 620 miles (1000 km). This is followed by more detached groups ranging from the Dolomites to the Pre-Alps, from the Apuane Alps to the Gran Sasso, and from Etna in Sicily to Gennargentu in Sardinia.

The physical and human geography of these mountain regions, however, is extraordinarily varied, giving rise to equally extraordinary and complex landscapes.

The heights of the 'white mountain' are characterized by a desert-like landscape. The closely-knit barriers of rock, the eternal glaciers and the thin air are an open rejection of human life; in such a sterile natural environment, in fact, not even plants and animals are able to survive for long. The 'green mountain,' on the other hand, embraces all forms of life. Here, to varying degrees according to the height, the flora and fauna thrive, while it offers human settlement, in its various forms, the possibility to survive in all seasons through agriculture and herding, indispensable resources for human life.

The altitude, the effects of the weather as the seasons bring intense cold, snow, wind and heavy rainfall, the short summers and the characteristic morphology of the territory have always represented an obstacle to man in his never-ending struggle against the natural elements of this particular environment.

The dangers of the elements in a mountain environment, in actual fact, should not be underestimated, as at times these can be devastating – severe thunderstorms, violent hailstorms and freezing cold, as well as landslides and avalanches make it even more difficult for man to settle in these regions.

Since the beginning of mankind, moreover, in order to survive mountain-dwellers have also had to defend themselves from their own species and from wild animals (though in the course of time they have succeeded in establishing to a certain extent their own supremacy).

238-239 The massif of Monte Ro-sa towers over the snow-covered expanse of the Po Valley.

In addition to this, through the centuries the geomorphology of the land has undergone considerable changes. The glaciers have become narrower, and the waters of the rivers and mountain streams have eroded the softer rock, defining the mountains and hills and making them crossable, and forming clefts, gorges and valleys. Thanks to this succession of natural events man gradually moved to the higher parts of the mountains, as far up as the vegetation reached, to settle in places that had once been perpetually covered with snow.

The mountains, therefore, were no longer seen only from a distance, lit up by the sun's rays or shrouded in cloud, and at a certain point in history man began to venture beyond them, urged by the need to expand. This need often took the form of peaceful trade or of emigration in search of more hospitable lands and more plentiful resources. Besides these noble motivations, however, many who crossed the mountain passes were driven by their thirst for power and wealth, frequently waging fierce wars and causing the death of a great many human beings for the sake of conquering other populations.

Roman historian Livy writes that, as far back as the 6th century, one hundred and fifty thousand Gauls led by Bellovesus first crossed the Alps near the Taurini mountain ridges and swarmed into the Po Valley, which was inhabited by the Etruscans.

Without doubt, however, the most famous exploit was the crossing made by Hannibal, who invaded Italy in 218 B.C. with a powerful army that included a great many horses and elephants, arriving perhaps by way of the Little St. Bernard or Mont Cenis passes. Subsequently, the Romans also used either these passes or that of Monginevro for the first time in 125 B.C. in order to reach the Gauls. Thus, thanks to Julius Caesar, the settlements of several of the Alpine populations began to be developed as, where before there had been only a few rough paths, the Romans began to plot a net-

work of roads, near which they built the *mansiones et mulationes* to provide accommodation and fresh horses for travelers, and the stationes as watch posts for guarding the areas, which were susceptible both to natural dangers such as landslides, snowstorms and bad weather in general, and to criminals, who could easily waylay travelers in such wild places.

In the Middle Ages the Alpine passes were crossed by hordes of barbarians arriving in Italy in search of spoils and fertile lands, despite the fact that, according to folk traditions, the mountains were considered evil places inhabited by dragons and terrible giants set to guard caves filled with gold and magnificent treasures, and by witches and demons (which replaced the earlier divinities of the Greeks and Romans). For many centuries travelers described their journeys through the Alps with a mixture of awe and repulsion, detesting all they saw and touched and regarding the mountains, as opposed to the lowlands, as an evil, hellish place. This idea was not entirely unforgivable, however, considering that the obstacle of the mountains had for thousands of years naturally isolated the various populations, along with their cultures.

With regard to the settlement of ancient civilizations in the mountains there are innumerable aspects, both positive and negative, relating to the fact that the psychological isolation of the mountain-dwellers created a close bond with the natural elements, despite their frequently violent manifestations.

While it is true that, being far removed from life on the plain, they remained somewhat out of touch with current events, at the same time the harsh mountain environment made them tougher, both in body and spirit, in their dealings with others. How many have found a safe refuge in the mountains in times of uncertainty, persecution, or war, rediscovering (in the case of those who settle there) a taste for freedom and independence? How many traditions, cultures and doctrines of conservation, moreover, have these uneducated mountain folk passed onto to us in an effort to teach respect for nature and to limit the exploitation of an environment that nowadays seems to be heading, slowly but surely, toward ecological disaster? Today many of these reflections may even make us smile, yet it is a fact that in the economy of mankind the mountain has always represented a constructive influence, and now, more than ever before, man is seeking to rediscover that primary condition of life, in order to gain a new freedom in his actions and his very existence.

Even though for a very long time the local people were far from favorable regarding the 'intrusion' of outsiders, today, thanks to the development of mountain tourism and the road systems, a great number of people come to the valleys of the 'green mountain' to stay in the small, quaint villages that nestle in the most beautiful landscapes. Here, in fact, at the beginning of the spring, after the last snow has melted, the woodlands, meadows and gorges give life to spectacular multicolored plants and flowers and the air is filled with their scent, while the mountain streams flow fast and furious, creating fantastic and unique shapes and forms along the way.

Once nature has fully awakened after its long winter hibernation the visitors arrive in search of peace or comfort, eager to be immersed in this enchanting natural environment, and although it has been said that "the beauty of the mountain is aggressive," each year the mountains continue to attract increasing numbers of people from all levels of society.

Modern times are evolving rapidly, with the consequent clear-cut transformation of social and economic wellbeing. Ever since the conquest of Monte Bianco on August 8, 1786, the inhabitants of the 'white mountain' (which for thousands of years was rightly considered an insurmountable obstacle and very dangerous to man) have witnessed the transformation, first through the discovery of mountain-climbing and later with the trend of skiing, of regions that were once abandoned and uninhabited into lively and extremely profitable areas.

240-241 Monte Pelmo, the impressive bulwark of Cadore, stands out against the sky like a gigantic sculpture.

242-243 The Pale di San Martino chain, in the southern Dolomites, is an extraordinary universe of rock, bounded by valleys, impenetrable passes and dense woodlands.

244-245 The heart of the Monte Bianco massif is an impressive maze of jagged spires and glaciers; standing out on the right is the Dente del Gigante (Giant's Tooth).

246-247 The village of Alagna, in Valsesia, shrouded in a thin blanket of cloud.

248-249 Framed by the enchanting forests of the Dolomites a stag majestically watches over its territory.

250 top   Monte Cristallo, in the eastern Dolomites, reaches a height of almost 990 ft (300 m).

250 bottom   The Lavaredo Peaks are part of the Dolomites of Sesto, situated at the north-eastern end of the Dolomites. The highest is the Cima Grande (Great Peak), in the center of the group, which reaches a height of 9839 ft (2999 m); following this is the Cima Ovest (West Peak), of a height of 9811 ft (2973 m), and the Cima Piccola (Small Peak), which reaches 9428 ft (2857 m)

251   The Pale di San Martino, near San Martino di Castrozza, bathed in the soft light of dawn.

Mountaintops in flight toward the sky

"The peaks that towered over us and the snow that separated them were colored in the most beautiful shades of pink and carmine; the entire horizon of Italy seemed to be encircled by a wide belt of purple and the full moon, tinged in the loveliest vermilion, rose above this band with the majesty of a queen."

H. B. de Saussure, *Voyages dans les Alpes.*

The bright cathedrals of the Dolomites of Brenta

Although the Brenta mountain chain, which originates to the west of the River Adda, is not actually part of the Dolomites, it is characterized by typical dolomitic features. Numerous ledges run horizontally along the high rocky walls, bearing witness to the long and incessant work of erosion carried out by time and the atmospheric agents. The central part of the chain, with its natural architectural creations, offers the most spectacular sights.

252 top The dizzying heights of the Brenta chain, tempered by a cloak of snow and the watercolor shades of sunlight.

252 bottom The peak of the Tosa ('Shearing'), so named for its 'cap' resembling a shorn head, is situated in the southern part of the Brenta chain, of which it is the highest peak 10,460 ft (3173 km).

253 The slopes of the Brenta chain bear witness to the most daring feats of European mountaineering history.

254-255 The jagged crest of the Crozzon of Brenta silhouetted against the background like a spectacular fan of rock.

256-257 The steep slopes of the Dolomites of Brenta form a long barrier of exceptional beauty.

258-259 The bold pinnacles of the Brenta chain inflamed by the light of the setting sun.

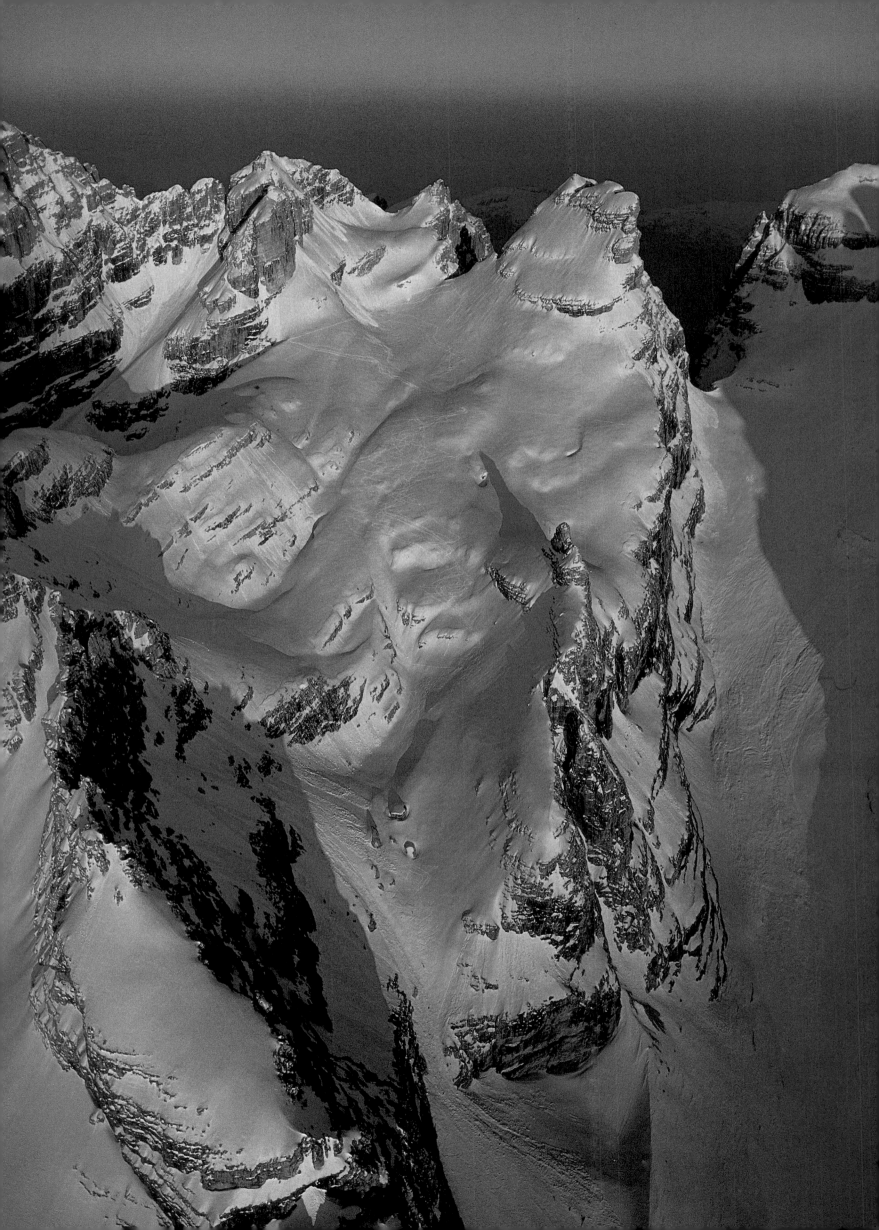

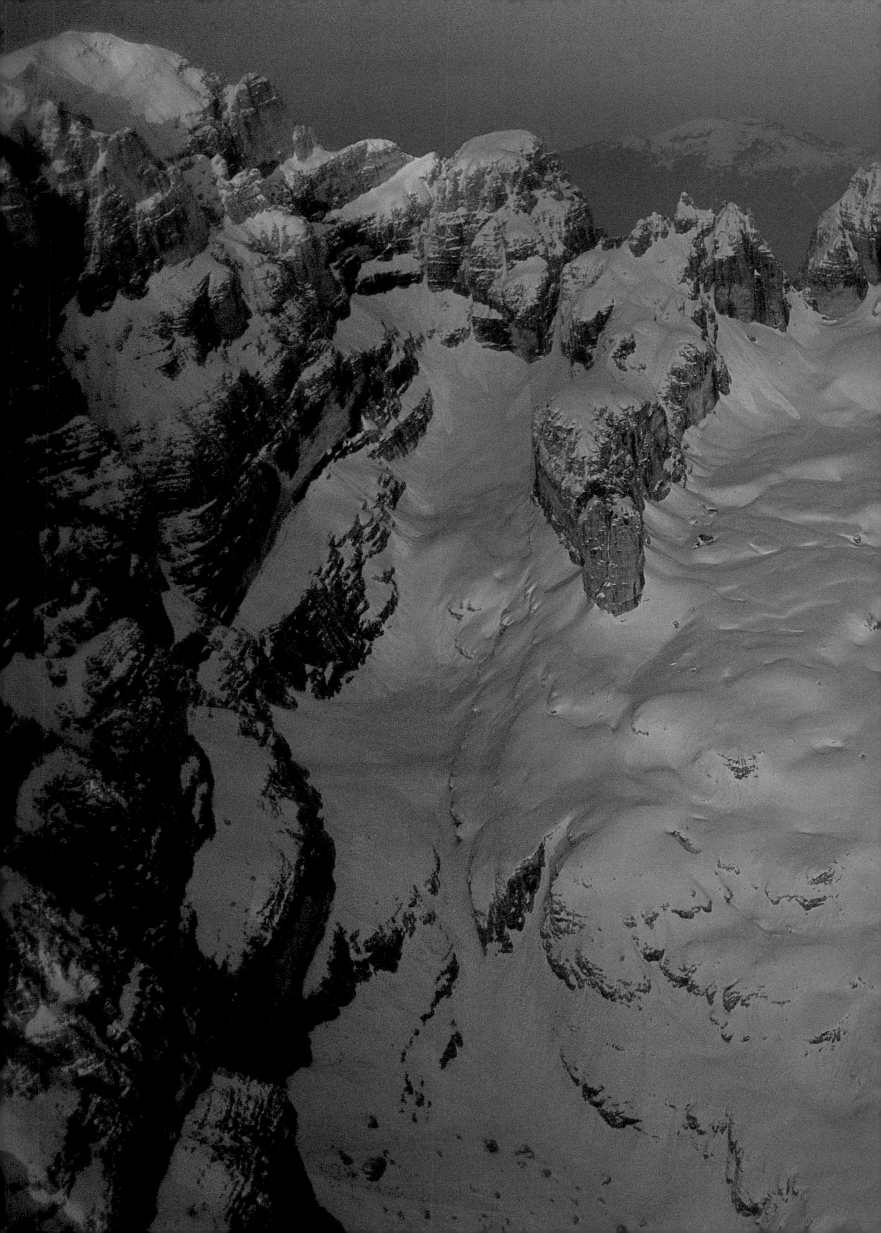

High altitude architecture

In a ring of incomparable splendor the chain embracing the Ampezzo basin, formed of huge solid rock faces and isolated mountains, represents a triumph of dolomitic rock. Particularly grand and majestic among these Ampezzan Dolomites is Monte Cristallo, while the ring ends at the west with the spectacular Tofana trio. The rock is characterized by an exceptional variety of forms, and the colors, ranging from yellow to red, from grey to black, take on iridescent hues in the alternation of sun and cloud.

260 left Up until the 1800s the magnificence of Monte Cristallo was known only to the inhabitants of the Ampezzo valley, and only became famous through the efforts of mountaineering pioneers.

260 top right The rock faces of the Tofana di Rozes and the Tofana di Mezzo are strongly characterized by tower-like formations and strange incisions. A cableway named 'Freccia del Cielo' (Sky Arrow) takes visitors up the Tofana di Mezzo to an observation post that commands a view of the entire Eastern Alps.

260 bottom right The Tofana di Rosez, considered to be the most spectacular of the three peaks known also as the 'Three Sisters,' reaches a height of 10,642 ft (3225 m).

261 The Tofana di Rozes resembles a huge temple carved out of the rock and supported by eight colossal pillars propelled toward the sky.

262 top Like an enchanted mountain Monte Cristallo emerges from its gossamer veil of cloud.

262-263 Not even the thick snow that covers its peaks is able to contain the powerful brightness of Monte Cristallo.

263 top Under the sun's rays the rocks come alive with an intricate web of golden light.

263 right Through the ages the wind and the weather have sculpted phantasmagorical sha-pes in the rock faces of Monte Cristallo.

Val Badia:
the heritage of a people

Val Badia was part of the Roman Rhaetia until it was seized by the Bavarians in the 6th century. In the year 814 it became part of the Kingdom of Hanover and, therefore, of the Holy Roman Empire. The Ladins of Val Badia today represent the last surviving echo of the area's Roman past. The complete Germanisation of these valleys, in fact, resulted in the ethnic isolation of the Ladins who, however, have steadfastly continued over the centuries to keep their language alive. Article 87 of the Statute of Trentino Alto Adige today guarantees the teaching of the Ladin language and the respect of Ladin culture and traditions; newspapers are printed also in Ladin, for example, and the local literature is flourishing.

264 The typical architecture of the Alto Adige Valley is characterized by supple and strongly vertical lines, like this bell tower in the village of La Villa.

264-265 The most ancient wing of the austere castle of San Martino, in Badia, dates back to the Middle Ages; several of the structures were partially rebuilt in 1600.

265 top left Under a veil of snow the village of Seres appears even more silent and snug.

265 top right Like a gigantic sleeping warrior the mountain overlooks the ancient village of Santa Croce.

*A long
and ancient journey*

Although today the ancient seasonal routine known as tranhumance (moving livestock from pasture to pasture) has virtually disappeared, it is still practiced in certain of the valleys of Alto Adige, such as Val Senales, from where the herdsmen set off with their flocks to go to Austrian pastures. Transhumance requires days and days of preparation. The journey is long, in fact, and the shepherds have to lead their flocks up the mountains along roads and paths that are not always practicable, often even with the prospect of crossing a glacier. The shepherd's whole family is involved in the enterprise, and it is always with great festivity and excitement that the flock is gathered together for the departure.

266 top The preparations for transhumance are long and complex; each member of the family has a set task in the arranging of the flock.

266 bottom The shepherd personally checks the health of the sheep and lambs to make sure problems will not arise during the journey.

266-267 The children wait eagerly for the moment of departure that for them marks the beginning of an exciting adventure.

267 top The flock is gathered together in an ordered fashion and each animal is marked with a distinguishing sign.

268-269 On the journey the dog, trusted companion of the shepherds, boldly faces the difficulties of transhumance as it watches over the flock.

*270 top The crossing of the gla-
cier is a sore test of the shepherd's strength.*

*270 bottom During the crossing
of the glacier the flocks and shepherds are sometimes temporarily
held up by sudden snowstorms.*

270-271 The clear blue sky and the sunlight sparkling on the snow are good omens and reassuring signs for the shepherds on their way to Austria.

271 top The everyday rhythms of nature continue uninterrupted even during the long journey of the transhumance.

*The Catinaccio,
a Rose Garden*

The Catinaccio, or Rosengarten (Rose Garden), was the legendary realm of King Laurino. According to Ladin folk tradition, this king lived in an immense palace on a mountain covered with roses, whose splendor could be seen throughout the valley. The king, infatuated with a beautiful princess named Similde, kidnaps the girl. Soon the soldiers sent by the father of the princess, following the trail, recognize the rose mountain, find the king and capture him. Before leaving the mountain Laurino casts a spell to punish his roses for 'betraying' him, transforming them into rocks so they would no longer see neither day nor night. From that day on, in fact, only at twilight is the Rose Garden once more seen to glow with an unearthly splendor.

272 The chain of the Catinaccio thrusts heavenward like a powerful bulwark. The dolomitic chain is bounded to the north by the Alpe di Siusi, to the east by Val di Fassa and to the west by Val di Tires.

273 A cascade of light floods the perennial snows on the Torri del Vaiolet. The three peaks are named after the first mountaineers who reached them (at the end of the last century): Delago, Stabeler and Winkler.

274-275 The last rays of the setting sun paint the peaks of the Torri del Vaiolet with a thousand iridescent shades.

276 The sunset reflected on the rocks of the Catinaccio, creating a spectacular light show that is repeated day after day, in all seasons, as soon as the sun lights up the mountains.

276-277 The stunning spectacle of a sea of fire washing the mountaintops of the Catinaccio chain recalls the legend of King Laurino.

277 top left The Germans use the name Alpenglühen ('Alpine lights'), and the Ladins the extremely romantic term of Enrosadita, to describe this extraordinary light phenomenon.

277 top right Like a spell that can only work when the conditions are right, the splendor of the Enrosadira can only be seen from the right place at the right time.

Sassolungo, the diamond of Val Gardena

It is difficult to find a mountain that can equal the Sassolungo ('Long Rock') in majesty and charm. Ascending the valley from Ortisei the shape of the 'Sasso' comes quickly into view, standing powerful and tall like an enormous totem. Only from the Gardena Pass, however, can we begin to get a glimpse of its length. The Sassolungo, in fact, with the immense crest of its eastern side, extends like a stone dragon for almost a mile (1.5 km). From Ortisei it is only necessary to climb as far as the little church of San Giacomo to be able to admire the mountain in all its splendor as it stands proudly displaying the impressive pillar of its tallest peak, while the entire spur stretches out with incomparable immensity.

278 The Sassolungo is the symbol of Val Gardena. Its 'plume,' which reaches a height of 10,497 ft (3181 m), can be seen even before arriving at Ortisei for those coming from the Valle dell'Isarco along the Strada Alta.

279 In the stretch between Ortisei and San Giacomo the Sassolungo displays in full its extremely complex and jagged mountainside in a classic picture of the Dolomites.

280 and 281 The mountains of the Sassolungo chain combine a majestic remoteness with an extraordinary assortment of shapes, qualifying them as some of the most spectacular peaks of the entire Dolomites.

The Dolomites are a revelation — surprisingly complex colossi of rock thrusting upward out of the pastures and expanses of green. The rugged world of the Dolomites is a solemn, marvelous world, characterized by rocky crests, white towers, spires and steeples. The penetrating charm of the white peaks arouses strong emotions; their appeal is the air, their beauty the dizzying heights. The Dolomites were named after the French geologist de Dolomieu, who analyzed their composition. The other name, the 'Pale Mountains,' was given to the mountain range by Carducci, and captures the characteristics of these lunar mountains set ablaze each time they are transformed by the Enrosadita.

Marmolada,
Queen of the Dolomites

The words of a Ladin song, *"O Marmolada, ti es regina* (O Marmolada, you are queen)," significantly express the sentiment of the local mountain population and suggest the wealth of myths and legends that have sprung up around this superb mountain which, in ancient times, was worshipped by the valley-dwellers who lived beneath it. In order to redeem it from this semi-pagan mythology, in fact, in 1804 an expedition made up of a lawyer, a doctor and a priest set off up the mountain to explore its untouched peak. One of the members of this expedition disappeared and was never found again, and not until half a century later was the peak finally conquered.

282 top The completeness of the Marmolada is truly unique, offering both marvelous rock faces for mountain climbing and opportunities for great skiing.

282 bottom In 1935 Günther Langes organized on the glacier of the Marmolada the first giant slalom competition in the history of ski touring.

283 Punta Rocca, the summit of the Marmolada, was conquered in 1860 by the expedition of John Ball, president of the British Alpine Club of London.

284-285 The Marmolada towers triumphantly over the peaks of the Dolomites at a height of over 11,028 ft (3342 m). Considering the enormous size of this majestic mountain it is easy to see why it has been nicknamed 'the Perfect Mountain.'

Val Badia:
two thousand years
of farming culture

Beneath the Dolomite's snow-capped peaks the countryside conceals a wealth of history and art. The small, neat Ladin villages, bear witness to the ancient mountain culture and the traditions of a farming population. Within the frame of an extraordinary natural environment can be found, almost as finishing touches to the landscape, the finest examples of mountain architecture, with ancient barns and granaries standing alongside the rustic *masi* (local farmhouses). Like tiny islands that have remained unchanged throughout the centuries, the villages of Alto Adige preserve the peace, simplicity and traditions of ancient times with great pride. Here the rhythm of the seasons still sets the pace of the everyday life of the Ladins, who adapt their habits and needs to the natural context in which they live.

286 The charming designs cut in the doors of the houses are the testimony of an ancient tradition of woodworking.

287 Still today the work of the local people is based on the rhythms of nature and the seasons.

288-289 The local farmhouses known as masi *are a characteristic aspect of the ancient villages of Alto Adige.*

The dolomitic walls
of the Sella

290-291 The straight-sided Sella Massif is crowned with an immense and bleak plateau.

291 top left The Sella, situated in the heart of the Dolomites, stands erect like a gigantic fortress.

291 top right The spectacular views of Sass Pordoi and Piz Boé are two of the most impressive of all the Dolomites.

292-293 The peak of Piz Boé, which stands at a height of 10,395 ft (3151 m), is the tallest of the chain.

294-295 The Sella is a vast and compact dolomitic massif with precipitous slopes and sheer pillars of rock.

296 The sharp points of the peaks of the Odle, situated in the north-western sector of the Dolomites, stretch upwards almost as if to touch the sky. The tallest of the peaks, Sass Rîgais, reaches a height of 9982 ft (3025 m).

297 The 'Cinque Torre di Aberau' ('Five Towers of Aberau'), in the Dolomites of Ampezzo, rule unchallenged over a boundless expanse of snow. The photo shows the Torre Grande (Great Tower) on the left, the Torre Sud (South Tower) in the center and the Torre Inglese (English Tower) on the right.

The fiery gothic spires of Pale di San Martino

The plateau of Pale di San Martino is a spectacular stony wasteland at a height of 8250 ft (2500 m), which takes its name from the most beautiful mountain of the group, the Pala ('Cliff') di San Martino. This impressive plateau stretches from east to west, with breathtaking sheer faces that plunge steeply down on either side. To the north the plateau is joined by a crest spiked with pinnacles, standing out among which are the jagged rocks known as the 'Torri della Pala.'

298 top The sparkling of the snow in the sun enhances the monumental complex of the Pale di San Martino.

298 bottom left The Pale di San Martino massif offers a wealth of spectacular views and perspectives. The Cima Vezzana and the Cimon della Pala are the main peaks of the central area. The latter, in particular, has been nicknamed the 'Matterhorn of the Dolomites' for its majestic size.

298 bottom right The rugged heights of the Pale chain softened by a white cloak of snow.

299 On a steep mountainside snow covers the sharp scales of rock, which the long and relentless process of erosion has shaped gradually over the ages.

300-301 *The Pale di San Martino swathed in white cloud. In order to preserve the extraordinary beauty of its mountain landscapes the chain was recently included in the National Park of Panaveggio-Pale di San Martino.*

302-303 *The majestic Castle of Tures is a symbol of the strength and prestige of the Tyrolese nobility.*

304-305 *This beautiful valley in the Val Gardena area is characterized by the deep green of its lush vegetation.*

Islands of
mountain culture

Perhaps the most fascinating appeal of the mountain is its snow-capped peaks, its boundless, white expanses glistening in the sun amidst pine trees and fir trees tipped with snow. Yet the gentle, sunny valleys that also characterize the mountain areas have a magic of their own, and it is especially in the sunshine of the spring and summer months that the valleys of Alto Adige fully reveal their greatest charm - an endless sea of green stretching out as far as the eye can see as it fades into a thousand emerald shades. The meadows and the pasture lands are scattered with tiny villages watched over by sharp, pointed church spires. Here, amongst the characteristic *masi* and the barns, the local farming communities live an intense and busy lives.

306 Wood is the symbol-element of Tyrolese tradition, as well as an immense resource for the mountain populations.

306-307 This magic scenario of Val Gardena seems to have been created by the brush of a painter.

307 top The gentle and sunny slopes of the Ladin valley of Livinallongo represent the ideal approach to the region's natural richness.

308-309 *The cold autumn fog descends on the ancient* masì *in Val Badia.*

In the mountains farming is a fundamental activity, closely bound to the life and culture of the valley people. It is hard and constant work, which through the seasons follows the unfaltering rhythms of nature. The environment and the weather conditions, moreover, make it necessary for the people to use all the resources available. In these modern times it is difficult for mountain farming to support itself, but in the Alto Adige it is protected in every possible way, partly for the sake of preserving a culture that is so essentially bound to an everyday life in close contact with nature.

An age-old tradition of celebration

The Ladin minorities are concentrated in the valleys around the foot of the dolomitic massif of the Sella. Badia, Gardena, Marebbe, Fassa, Livinallongo and Ampezza represent the strongholds of an ancient culture that not even the onslaught of tourists has succeeded in changing or weakening. The Ladins are essentially farmers and breeders, and have developed a philosophy of life that is based on accepting whatever nature brings their way.

312 During the first ten days of June the Ladin people celebrate the Sacro Cuore di Gesù (Sacred Heart of Jesus) with a traditional procession that takes place in Val Badia.

313 An important (and compulsory) feature of the procession is the characteristic local costume, which is worn with pride by all the valley-dwellers.

316-317 In Val Badia, situated at the center of the Sella Mountains in the Dolomites of Alto Adige, the Ladin community cultivates its ancient traditions with great pride. In the photo, taken during the Procession of the Sacred Heart of Jesus, local village folk parade in twos through the meadows, dressed in traditional costume.

318-319 The silent industriousness of work in the fields does not disturb the peace of the natural environment.

The titans of light

The Monti Pallidi (Pale Mountains) owe their mysterious appearance to a succession of geological processes that began over two hundred million years ago. In those days the dolomitic area rested on an enormous slab of porphyritic rock produced by volcanic eruptions. The landscape was bare and full of toxic gases. Over millions of years the vast lagoons gradually lowered and gave way to a shallow sea, in which the work of the coral contributed to the sedimentation of seaweed and molluscs. With the movement of the sea there then began the process of modeling the dolomitic chains until the glaciation of the Quaternary Period, like an immense scalpel, gave the mountains a last powerful 'filing.'

320-321 *The blazing crest of the Sassolungo dominates the Alpe di Siusi.*

321 top *A band of light exalts the solemn profile of the Piz Boé.*

322-323 All the mighty power of nature is expressed in the colossal embrace of the Sasso della Croce.

323 The fiery evening sun illuminates fantastic perspectives on the Pale di San Martino chain.

324-325 The breathtaking beauty of the Cimon della Pala, the most representative peak of the Pale di San Martino, cannot help but lift the spirit up toward the mysteries of the Absolute.

326 The Dolomites of the Valley of Agordo guard an untouched white strip of paradise.

327 Nature speaks the mystic language of the divine, and the mystery reveals itself to the spirit.

328-329 The purity and strength of asceticism are manifest in the skyward thrust of the peaks. In the photo the peaks of the Alpi Giulie seem almost to merge with the intense blue of the surrounding sky.

*The fairytale forest
of Tarvisio*

Between the most easterly part of the Alpi Carniche and the northern chain of the Alpi Giulie extends an area of around 100,000 acres (40,000 hectares) covered with lush alpine forest. Originally owned by the Church and later by Austria, this immense woodland became Italian property just before the end of the First World War. The Tarvisio forest boasts a rich plant and animal population, with firs, pines, larches, beeches and sycamores sharing a perfect natural habitat with deer, roe deer, chamois, martens, eagles and grouse — a true triumph of nature that makes the Tarvisio forest an almost enchanted place.

330 Thanks to the constant watchful presence of the foresters from the early 11th century up until today and the good conservation of the environment, the area is rich in animal life.

330-331 The Lake Fusine seems almost to be watched over and protected by the huge massif of the Mangart.

331 top left Hazy watercolor shades characterize this evocative view of the forest veiled in fog.

331 top right During the spring thaw, one of the liveliest events in the forest, nature reawakens and all the creatures prepare for the coming of the season of new life.

332 top The naturalistic, ecological, cultural and historical significance that the Tarvisio Forest incarnates is extremely profound. In it, in fact, are condensed three climatic zones – the Mediterranean, the Continental and the Oceanic zones.

332 bottom The ancient houses of Camporosso fit perfectly with the fairytale atmosphere of the forest.

333 The Tarvisio forest may truly be called a European forest. Not only does it extend across various geographic areas of Europe, in fact, but it also brings together three different European races – the Italians, the Germans and the Slavs.

334-335 A dense pine forest encircles the Lake Fusine, near Tarvisio.

The white sea

The Ortles massif stands in the Central Alps of the Retiche chain; it is generally referred to as including also the Cevedale chain and known as the Ortles-Cevedale chain. The mountains are surrounded by four beautiful valleys – Val Venosta, Valle d'Ultimo, Val di Sol and Valtellina, which, in turn, are characterized by four rivers – the Adige, the Valsura, the Noce and the Adda. Due to its extent and its many glaciers, the Ortles-Cevedale chain is considered the largest mountain complex of Trentino Alto Adige. Here, in 1935, the Stelvio National Park was founded, covering an area of 520 sq. miles (134,620 hectares) that includes the Ortles-Ceve-dale chain and a great many valleys.

336 top The town of Livigno, situated at the end of a valley at a height of 5940 ft (1800 m), is an extremely popular holiday and winter sports location.

336 bottom Snowfields and glaciers are a fundamental element of the morphology of the Ortles-Cevedale massif.

337 The snow's stunning brightness transforms the peaks of the Ortles-Cevedale chain into gigantic icebergs stretching up to the sky.

338-339 Many peaks of the Ortles-Cevedale massif exceed a height of almost 10,000 ft (3000 m), such as those of Trafoi, Gran Zebrù, Cevedale, Vioz and the Corno dei Tre Signori.

The industrious valley

Between these mountains, in a pleasant valley crossed by the river Adda, the region of Valtellina is a hive of industry, and a generous land that is able to draw from its inhabitants the truly great resources of the local economy. The people of Valtellina are fiercely proud of their cultural and historical heritage, which they preserve with passionate dedication. The nature trails that lead visitors through its parks and up to its peaks cross paths with quite different, yet no less appealing, itineraries – those of the local gastronomy and the winemaking culture, activities that take place in the old chalets and so-called *crotti* (natural caves).

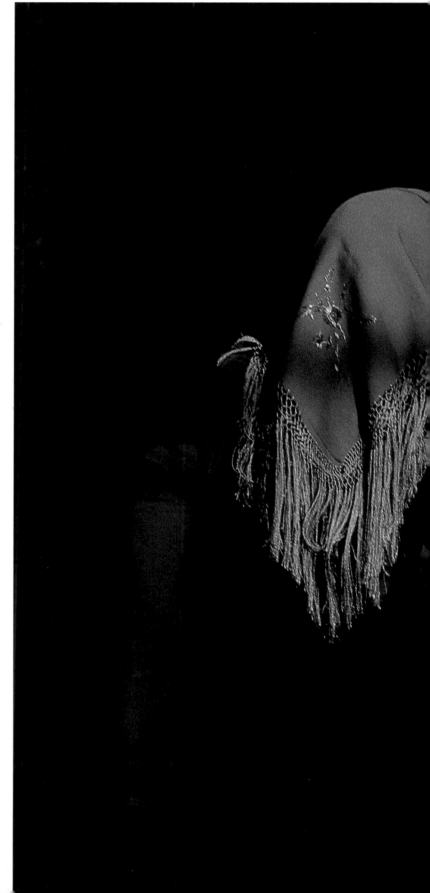

340 top Polenta is a traditional dish of the Valtellina area.

340-341 The richly embroidered shawl is one of the most typical accessories of the women's traditional costume, which is still worn on Sundays and holidays.

341 top left A curious feature of the town of Chiavenna are the crotti, natural caves that are ventilated by drafts known as sorel, *which enter through clefts in the rock and contribute to maintaining a constant temperature, ideal for the storage of wines and cheeses.*

341 top right In Valtellina a typical and ancient industry that still flourishes today is the weaving of rugs known as pezzotti. *In the past, old coats and jackets were cut into shreds and transformed into blankets and rugs; today the* pezzotto *is considered a true art object.*

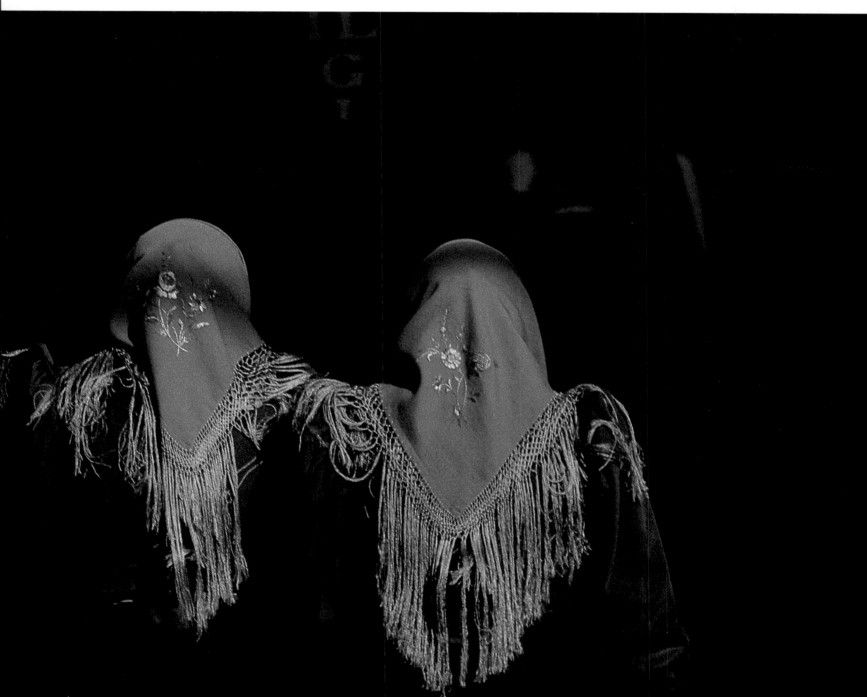

The strength of tradition

The Valtellina's natural remoteness represents a real bulwark against any outside intrusion, and the customs and traditions of the past remain unchanged. In villages and small towns like Grosio and Ravoledo the women wear their traditional costumes in everyday life, and the community still bases its economy on the resources that earth and nature offer.

342 The traditional fancy-dress costume known as 'Bernarda' animates the merry carnival of the Valtellina.

342-343 The traditional figures of the white bear and tamer parade through the streets of Grosio during the carnival. The characters recall the ancient tales and legends of the mountains of the Valtellina.

343 top *The 'Magra Quaresima' and the 'Paralitico' are two other grotesque figures that take part in the carnival parades of Grosio.*

344 The most evocative cere-
monies of the entire Valtellina region are those organized in
Bormio for the Easter festivities.
On the occasion of the so-called
'Pasquali' celebrations Bormio's
village square is thronged with
people eager to watch the traditional procession.

345 During the 'Pasquali' celebrations it is common to see in the
streets of Bormio picturesque
characters sporting long beards
and impeccable in their traditional
costumes, unexpected symbols of
a culture that is strongly connected with the land and deeply rooted in the hearts of the people.

346-347 The faces of the local children reflect clearly the benefits of a healthy mountain life.

347 The children are also dressed in traditional costume for the 'Pasquali' festivities.

Sparkling peaks

348 The Ortles-Cevedale massif stands out in a lunar landscape of white expanses of snow.

349 The snow-covered dunes of Monte Cevadale sparkle with reflected crystalline light.

350-351 The titanic Monte Ortles towers over the other peaks of the mountain chain.

The Presanella massif characterizes the mountain chains of western Trentino. The encircling chain, with its extremely rugged and complex peaks, opens between Val di Genova and Val di Sol, in the point where the Presanella chain meets the Presena Pass. Many of the crests exceed 10,000 ft (3000 m) in height, with the highest, from which the chain takes its name, reaching 11,550 ft (3500 m). The morphology of the massif is characterized by numerous saw-toothed crests, twisting glaciers, wide ca-nyons and steep moraines.

352 The shadows lengthen on the snow-covered slopes, creating strong contrasts of light.

353 A thick cloak of snow draws patterns and sculpts white shapes on the rock faces.

354 top Valsesia is the repository of ancient traditions, never forgotten, which are renewed from season to season. Its processions, flower arrangements and costumes all bear witness to this heritage. The Walser minority ethnic group in particular keeps alive its noble past, protecting it from the ravages of modern times.

354 The medieval Fénis castle is probably the most resistant to the rigors of the weather in the Val d'Aosta. It was built from 12th-15th centuries near the village of the same name in the Dora valley. Still standing are the solid rectangular towers, the more slender circular tower and the crenellated walls.

Peaks and castles

The enormous bulk of Monte Bianco, seen from the Freney wall, is recognizable by the large glacier where the Bonatti expedition made its dramatic attempt at a descent in 1961.

The pearl of Valsesia

Nestled in a valley of Val Grande in Valsesia is the charming little town of Alagna, the main settlement of the Valsesia region and an important weather station, as well as a famous tourist center for the numerous mountain excursions that the Monte Rosa chain offers mountain-climbers of all levels. The trails of Alagna have an ancient history – in the 13th century, in fact, a population from Vallese crossed the Alps and settled in the various villages of the area. The Walser population still preserves today, at least partly, its ancient dialect, which is very similar to German.

356 Snow falling in large flakes is a constant presence in the winters of Valsesia.

356-357 This evocative setting emphasizes the typical chalet architecture of Alagna.

357 top left This surreal world of whiteness will not change until the first warmth of spring slowly begins to melt it away.

357 top right The tiny hamlet of Pedemonte covered in a soft white blanket.

358-359 A fleeting patch of brightness lights up the Monte Rosa massif above Alagna.

Valsesia:

a taste of the past

The handicraft traditions and the customs and usages of Valsesia are a living testimony of the history of this mountain population. The memory of a difficult life lived at the foot of the mountains is expressed in the plain-spoken language of the people and, above all, in the fine small handicraft objects that contain all their love for the mountain and for the local tradition, which is made up of stories, legends and everyday adventures on the peaks and glaciers. Maintaining the old customs of bygone days and the ancient wisdom of the mountains means keeping alive a bond with the past that dates back to the 1400s, when several German-speaking Walser communities crossed the passes from Switzerland and settled in this charming valley at the foot of Monte Rosa.

360 The art of woodcarving is still passed down in the villages of Valsesia.

360-361 The typical Valsesian chalets bear witness to the ancient living traditions of the mountain people.

361 top left A woman walks with slow and rhythmic pace, bent under the weight of a hay-filled pannier.

361 top right Cattlesheds and barns are still the setting for a large part of the mountain people's work.

362 In many areas of the valley, people are still actively involved in farming activities, especially the harvesting of hay, as in this mountain pasture near the village of Rossa.

362-363 The pannier and the rake are inseparable companions during the hay harvest.

Monte Rosa,
the cradle of dawn

364 The name of Monte Rosa is thought to derive either from the Celtic Ros, which means 'peak' or 'horn,' or from the word Roise, which, in the dialect of the Val d'Aosta, means 'glacier;' in this case, Monte Rosa would mean 'Mountain of Glaciers.'

365 In the not-too-distant past the people of Alagna believed that the souls of the departed, before rising up to heaven, were obliged to spend a period of time in the glaciers of Monte Rosa, in order to purge themselves of their lesser sins.

366-367 The silhouette of the Capanna Margherita stands out on the rocky crest of Monte Rosa. Since it opened on August 18th, 1993 the refuge has undergone a number of restorations, the most recent of which was completed in 1980. The present structure contains 15 rooms and sleeps 70 people.

368-369 A surreal light accentuates the unearthly size of these peaks. The Rosa massif culminates with the Punta Dufour which, after Monte Bianco, is Europe's highest peak.

370-371 The Dufour crest of Monte Rosa at dawn.

Ice Sculptures

372 and 372-373 Fantastic shapes sculpted in the glaciers of Monte Rosa.

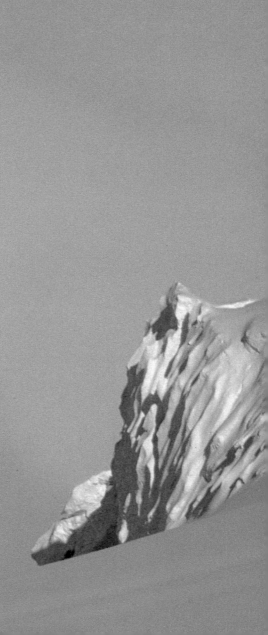

374-375 A huge glacier leads the roped party up to the peaks of Monte Rosa.

375 top The Capanna Margherita emerges like a mirage from a boundless desert of snow.

376 A peak of the Monte Rosa chain rises above a sea of cloud.

377 The glacier offers disquieting spectacles of extremely deep crevices and walls of ice.

378-379 Nature expresses all its awesome power in the colossal remoteness of the Vincent Pyramid.

*The retention
of ancient practices*

Geography, history, environment and customs – a marvellous fusion created over centuries that results today in the unexpected discovery of fragments from the distant past. Valsesia is a rich land, where even the delightful hospitality of the local inhabitants is tradition, and where the habits and customs seem to emerge from a late-19th-century print. The only harsh aspect of Valsesia life is the climate, which goes from the gentle warmth of the vineyards to the frozen mass of the glacier. Yet the snow-covered peaks, where the chamois skip among the rocks and the marmots squeal, hold within them the warm heart of a people for which simplicity and openness have become a tradition.

380 A woman dressed in the traditional local costume spins wool using the method still commonly practised in the homes of Valsesia.

380-381 A rustic chalet brightened up by colorful geraniums.

381 top left Valsesian women embroider their own shawls and ribbons that decorate their costumes.

381 top right Insets of finely-worked lace and embroidery decorate the costumes of the Val Fobello.

382 The recipes for making butter and cheese are handed down to the young girls as a valuable heritage of home economics.

383 The colors of the mountain flowers brighten up the embroidery of the costumes of the Val Carcoforo.

Rosario Fiorito:
the miracle of God
and the prayers of man

Every year, in the month of May, the Procession of the Rosario Fiorito ('Flowering Rosary') takes place in the village of Alagna. Wearing traditional dress, the inhabitants of the village follow the procession as it leads up a long and picturesque path through meadows and across streams, carrying ancient standards and a statue of the Madonna. The majestic backdrop of unspoiled nature emphasizes the harmonious aspect of the religious ceremony, and the chain of mountains all around becomes a magnificent setting in which customs and rituals that are so deeply rooted in the hearts of the faithful are enacted.

A crown of mountains
for the bride

386 top In the parish church of Rossa one of the rare weddings in traditional Valsesian dress is celebrated.

386 bottom The wedding procession makes its way peacefully toward the church against a charming backdrop of pines and firs.

387 The bride's dress is a true masterpiece of fine handicraft – it took over a year, in fact, to complete the weaving, dying and embroidering of the fabrics.

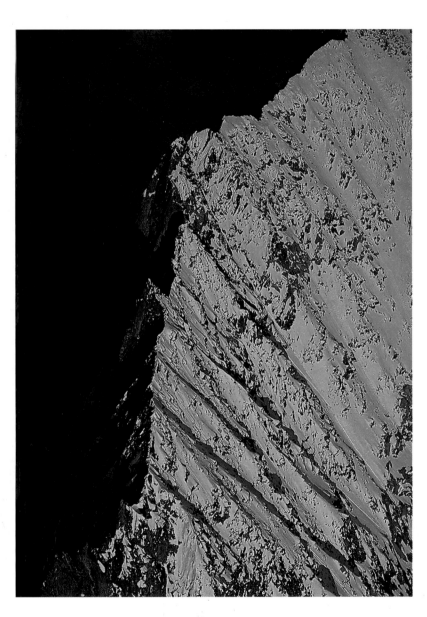

388 The sheer slope of the Grandes Jorasses, part of the Monte Bianco chain, plunges dizzily down toward the valley.

388-389 The variety and boldness of alpine architecture creates constantly changing impressions. The rib of the Grandes Jorasses thrusts upward out of the endless rocky waves; in the distance can be seen the profiles of the Matterhorn and Monte Rosa.

389 top The extraordinary wall of the Grandes Jorasses marks the boundary between France and Italy; in the background is the barrier of the Drus mountains.

390-391 The awesome sight of the innumerable isolated peaks, standing out among which is the Dente del Gigante (Giant's Tooth), surpasses all imagination.

392-393 Unearthly and fantastic, the peak of Monte Bianco is beyond the range of all common measure.

Needles of rock

394 top Before the colossal spectacle of the Grandes Jorasses the spirit is silenced and the thoughts transmute, just as with each step the rock is transformed, changing shape and color.

394 bottom An evocative view of the Monte Bianco massif as seen from the Val Ferret.

395 The magnificent Aiguille Noire appears, in its arrangement and the angle of its spurs, to be relentlessly reaching up toward the sky. The peak, which is part of the Monte Bianco chain, overlooks Val Veny.

The glaciers,
crystalline fields of ice

396 top To mountain-climbers the glacier is always an exciting experience, a direct confrontation with the severe nature of the mountain. Shown here is a view of the glacier of Gran Paradiso.

396-397 The blinding white of the glacier of Monte Bianco seems to claim the inviolability of the peaks.

397 top Deep seracs score the rough surface of the Lys glacier on Monte Rosa.

397 right Erosion creates inlays and graffiti on the icy walls of Monte Bianco.

398-399 Abstract patterns and engravings in the ice are the only imprints to be seen in this uncontaminated world.

400-401 A roped party making its way toward Monte Rosa.

The colossal bulk of the glaciers ploughs into the valley, eroding it and carving vast cavities. Through the centuries the eternal ice smoothes and levels out the ground and draws veins and intricate patterns, giving the rocky bed its characteristic 'sheep's hump' appearance. The relentless erosive action of the glaciers is also responsible for the so-called 'potholes' or 'giant's cauldrons,' which are deep caves with extremely smooth and sparkling walls.

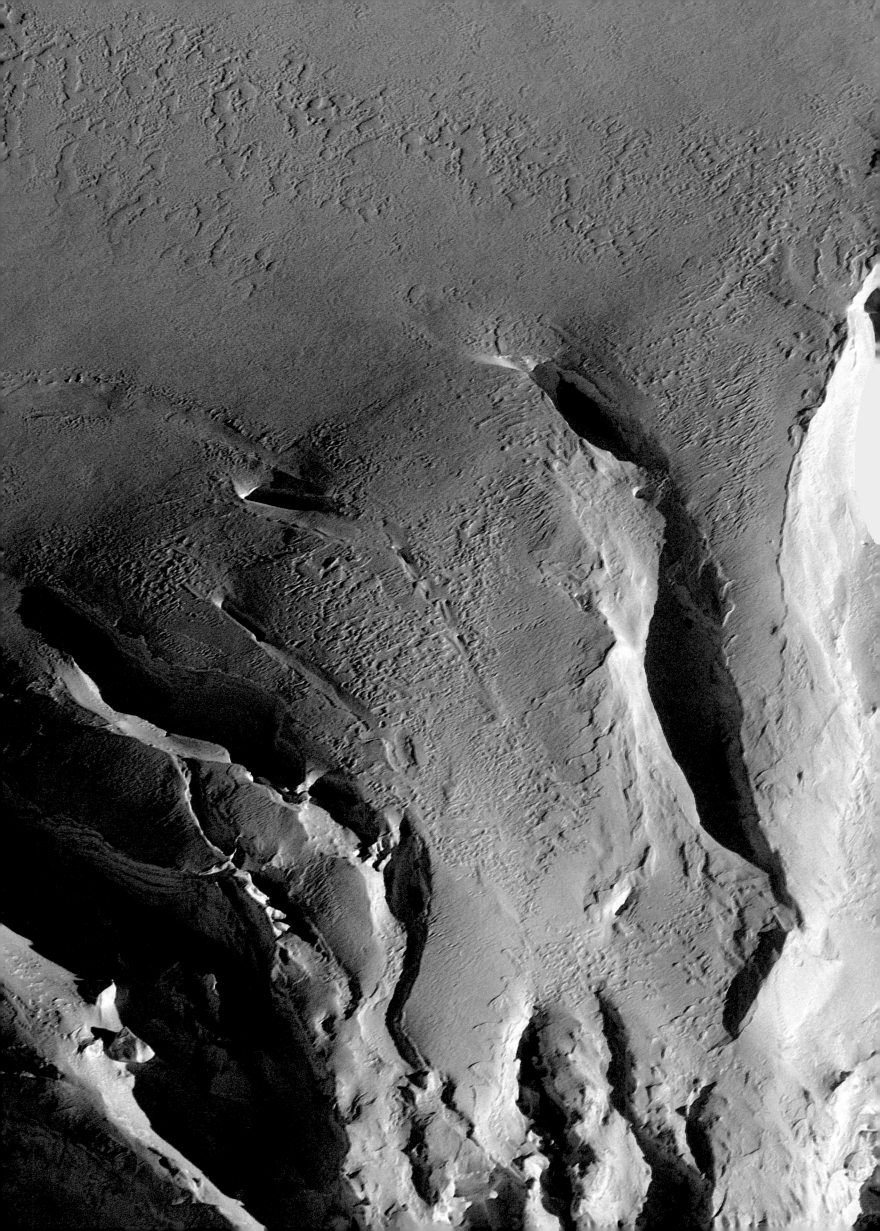

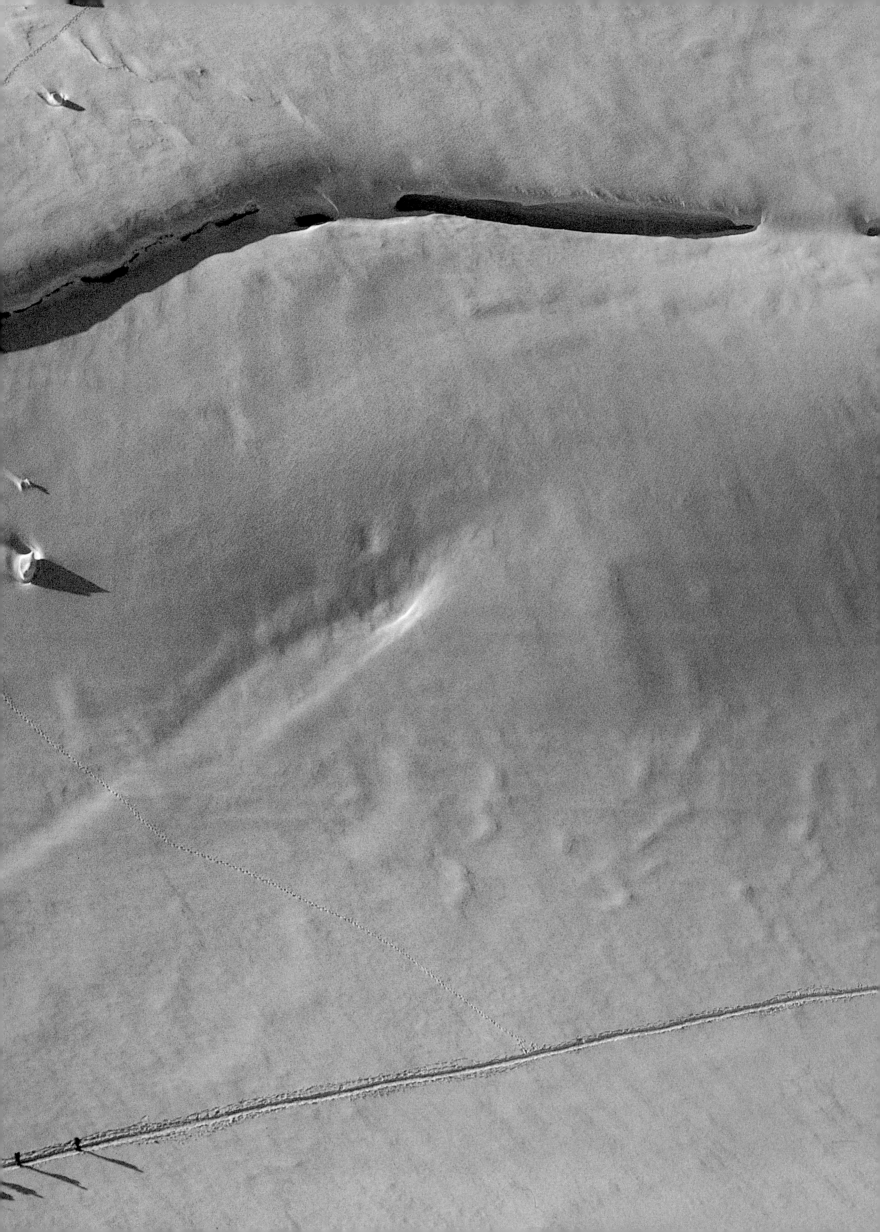

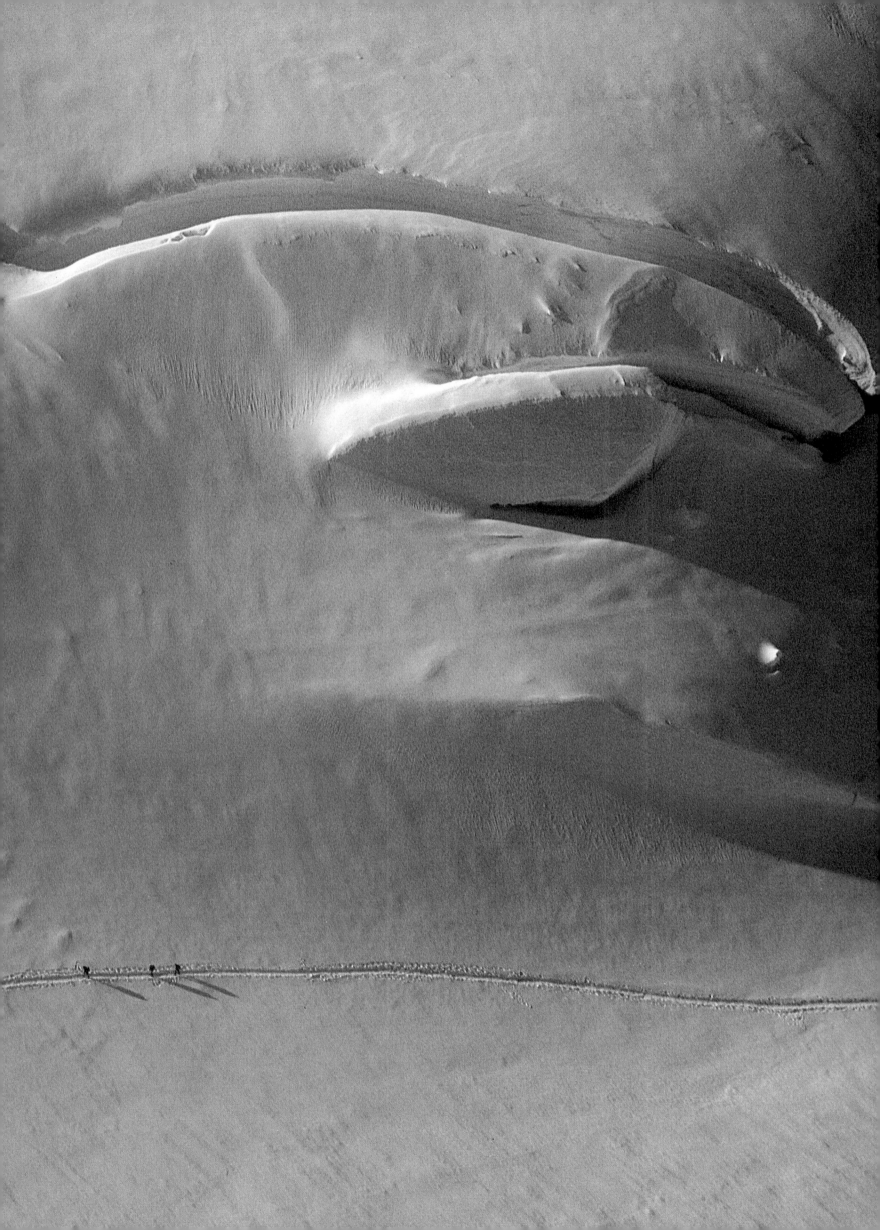

Val d'Aosta:
natural masterpieces,
historical treasures

402 In spite of the first snows of winter nature still retains the warmth of its soft and transparent shades.

403   *In its unchanging pureness the magnificent chain around the Val d'Aosta proclaims the eternal values of nature.*

In the chalets and the mountain pastures the simple and traditional dairy industry that has been practiced among the inhabitants since ancient times has today become a highly prized and appreciated. The preparation of butter and cheeses (especially the typical *fontina*) through long and complex processes calls to mind an ancient world based on nature and simplicity. The secrets and rarest recipes, and the loving care dedicated to these activities, emerge in the everyday gestures that betray the inseparable bond of the people with their sound, time-honored values.

406 Butter-making requires precise and careful attention, and the secrets of producing a genuine product are well known to all the mountain folk.

407 Ancient rituals and flavors find their element in the simplicity of a chalet and the company of a local cheese expert.

Battle of the queens

One of the lesser known but equally interesting folk events is the cow-fighting competition, which is held in Cogne and other towns of Val d'Aosta every Sunday from April to October, when the final is held. In the *Luttes des Reines* ('Battles of the Queens') the leaders of the herds (those wearing cow-bells) face each other in a short and quiet yet powerful horn-to-horn battle, until the weaker of the two withdraws, surrenders and is eliminated from the competition. Breeders, local villagers and townsfolk, as well as a great number of tourists, participate enthusiastically in the fights.

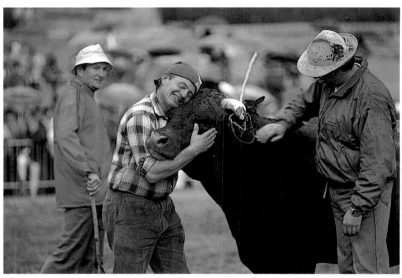

*The mountains
of Val d'Aosta,
open books of stone*

410 A dark and mysterious atmosphere seems to call up the ancient legends that have built up around the peak of the Aiguille Noire.

411 The sinister light of a storm
briefly illuminates the peaks of the
Val di Rhêmes, part of the Gran
Paradiso chain.

412 On the side facing Val d'Aosta the summit of Monte Cervino (Matterhorn), which reaches a height of 14,778 ft (4478 m), is not characterized by the jagged roughness of other mountains but displays a truly surprising and striking gracefulness.

412-413 The Matterhorn resembles an immense and almost perpendicular tower, whose sides plunge headlong down into the abyss.

414-415 The pyramid of the Matterhorn stands out in an immense, barbed panorama of mountains, glaciers and pinnacles, each separated from the others by hazy and indefinable distances.

*Gran Paradiso,
the freedom of high
altitudes*

*Gran Paradiso,
the freedom of high
altitudes*

Gran Paradiso National Park, situated in the Graie Alps at a height ranging from 4000 ft (1200 m) to 13,200 ft (4000 m), was founded in 1922, the first of all the Italian parks. In this period the ibex, or rock goat, risked extinction, and it is only thanks to a diligent conservation program that today the region boasts an ibex population of almost 4000. The Park, which covers an area of 173,000 acres (70,000 hectares), also provides protection for 6000 chamois, mountain hares, marmots and stoats, not to mention as many as 1500 different plant species, which thrive in the Paradisia Alpine Botanic Garden that covers an area of 12,000 sq. ft (10,000 sq. m).

416 Perfectly camouflaged against the white snow, the shape of a mountain hare is barely distinguishable.

416-417 The spectacular snow-covered crest of Gran Paradiso stands out sharply against the background, contrasting with the fluffiness of the clouds.

417 top The brisk movements of a stoat betray its presence among the white expanse of snow.

417 right The rocks and forests of Gran Paradiso are a perfect refuge and breeding ground for the alpine chamois and the black grouse.

417

418 top *For the ibex the mating season is a long process of courting and pursuit among the slopes and crags of the mountains.*

418 bottom *The alpine chamois generally lives in herds. While the group grazes the leader moves to a higher position, from where it can keep watch over the area. In case of danger it warns the herd by letting out a clear, sharp whistle.*

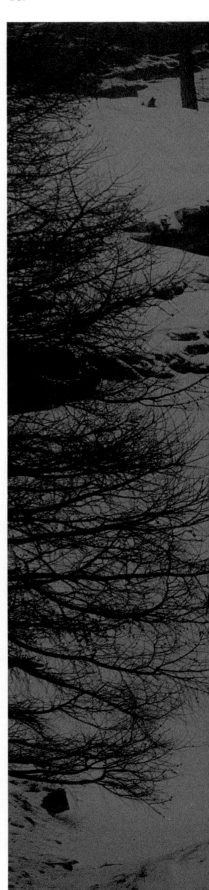

418-419 A fox and a group of ibex study each other at close range.

419 top The golden eagle is without doubt the most powerful and feared bird of prey that nests among the rocks of the Gran Paradiso.

420-421 The Gran Paradiso massif stretches out its broad slope characterized by rocky spurs and pinnacles.

422-423 The forests sleep in the silence of winter, as they conceal beneath their still dull and hazy colors the dens and lairs of hibernating animals.

424 top The alpine chamois grazes on the grassy plateau during the summer, while in winter it feeds on grass and roots and shelters in the caves beneath the overhanging rocks.

424-425 Larch woods set ablaze with the warm red shades of fall.

425 top A stoat pokes a curious head out of its hole.

425 right Proud and majestic, the ibex is not daunted by the mountain's dizzying height or sheer precipices.

*A peaceful world
of dances, games and
wholehearted dedication*

426-427 The typical mountain houses with their characteristic slated roofs are a recognized symbol of the alpine village.

427 top In the fall the mountain landscapes are tinged with the most spectacular colors.

In the mountains the carnival generally recalls old folk customs that date back to the days when the different districts were in constant competition with each other. Banners and standards display heraldic coats-of-arms and images of castles, symbols of a medieval past full of historical events and characters. Children and adults alike are caught up in the general euphoria that spreads through the streets and squares of the town.

The traditional costumes of the Valle di Gressoney are particularly rich in elaborate embroidery and trimmings. The rigid headdress worn by the women and girls, decorated with ribbons and corners embroidered in gold thread, is a fine example of the skill with which the women of Val d'Aosta fashion these characteristic costumes. The local festivities, which are held in the main village squares or in some appropriate grassy clearing, represent a real tourist attraction, as well as a spectacular combination of color and music.

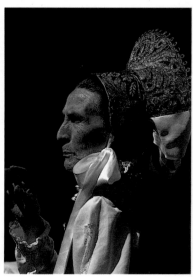

432-433 The thrill of flying, experienced between gorges and mountain peaks on board a hang-glider.

433 top The helicopter is the fastest and most efficient way to reach even the highest and most difficult peaks.

433 bottom A leap into space, surrounded by the incomparable alpine chain.

*Val d'Aosta,
a land of chalets
and castles*

434 Small rustic chalets, half-secluded in a dense forest of snow-covered firs. It is not difficult to imaging the warm and cosy atmosphere in which the simple indoor rituals of everyday life are performed.

435 Beneath a white blanket of snow the tiny village of Valsavaranche seems to be sleeping, but, in actual fact, inside the houses the inhabitants are already preparing for the coming springtime labors.

436 Like in a fairy tale the turrets of a castle can be seen rising out of the dense forest. The Castle of Savoy is situated at Gressoney-St. Jean.

436-437 Time and history appear not to have damaged the pride of the Castle of Graines, which stands in solemn memory of its bygone medieval glory.

438-439 The thick cloud creates an illusion of photomontage in this picture of the Castle of Introd, swathed as if by magic in a gauzy blanket.

440 top *The mountain Gran Sasso stands in the middle of the Abruzzi Apennine mountains; its highest peak is the Corno Grande at 9560 ft (2868 m). Its slopes are covered with vegetation right up to the snowline. Grains and fruits are cultivated on the mountain's sides and cattle, sheep and goats are raised in the meadows for the production of cheese and other dairy items.*

440 bottom *The Sybilline mountains in the central Apennine chain are a watershed between the Tyrrhenian and Adriatic seas. Their highest point is at Mount Vettore at 8123 ft (2437 m) At the feet of these mountains, wide plains open out where a carpet of brightly colored flowers appears as soon as the snows melt so that they are in full flower at the start of summer.*

The mysterious peaks of the Appennines

441 In the quietest moments, the summit of Monte Etna can easily resemble the one of any other mountain. This volcano, however, is one of the most active on Earth.

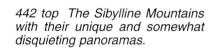
The Sibylline
Mountains,
home of legend and lore

442 top The Sibylline Mountains with their unique and somewhat disquieting panoramas.

442-443 The mysterious peaks of the Sibylline Mountains recall ancient legends and folklore.

443 top *Castelluccio, a tiny picturesque hamlet of Norcia, is famous for the extremely good lentils that grow in the fields at the foot of the village.*

443 right *In the morphology of the Sibylline Mountains steep-sided ravines and narrow gorges alternate with gentle slopes sculpted by glaciers.*

The Sibylline mountain chain is situated in the heart of the central Apennines between the southern Marches and Umbria, dominating both the Tyrrhenian and Adriatic seas. For its role as watershed between these two seas, in fact, the mountain chain may well be considered the barycenter of the Italian peninsula. It is, perhaps, due to its geographic position that, in the medieval literature that grew up around Italian folk traditions, Monte Sibilla was the home of the Virgilian prophetess known as the Apennine Sibyl, who lived in a magnificent palace at the entrance to the Underworld. A great many writers were also inspired by the local legends, including Andrea da Barberino and Antoine de La Salle.

444 *The Piana Grande, ('Great Plain') of Castelluccio, stretching out at the foot of Monte Vettore.*

445 *Sheep-farming is the basis of the Sibylline economy.*

At the foot of these moun- tains are boundless expans- es of meadowland, which are covered with snow for a good part of the year. The eye sweeps over an endless succession of hills and plains, which, on clear days, can be seen fading gradual- ly away down to the sea. Im- mediately above this gently receding landscape, emerg- ing like giants out of a light veil of mist, are the main mountain chains of Central Italy – the Gran Sasso, the Terminillo, the Maiella, the Amiata and the Subasio. Af- ter the spring thaw, the plains become covered with flowers, whose colors and shades change from one week to the next until they reach the height of their splendor at the beginning of summer.

Gran Sasso:
the powerful guardian
of the Apennines

The Gran Sasso limestone massif is located in the central part of the Abruzzi Apennines, overlooking the Adriatic coast. The massif is actually made up of two parallel chains joined together by huge transversal ribs, while the most striking feature is the endless succession of scattered pinnacles and tall peaks. The perspectives, therefore, are infinite, and each one offers views that are truly stunning, from brilliant white snowfields (the most important of which being that of Monte Corno) to wide expanses sloping down toward green pastures and sheer precipices. On the mountainsides, reaching almost up to the snow line, grows an extremely rich alpine vegetation.

448 top A view of an immense mountainside near the Camosciara, standing out against the blue sky.

448 bottom The Corno Piccolo ('Little Horn'), so called to distinguish it from the Corno Grande, offers one of the most charming panoramas of the Abruzzo massif.

449 The undulating peak of the Scindarella dusted with white after a light snow shower.

450-451 Sunset over the vast plain of Campo Imperatore.

The Abruzzo National Park: a green lung in the heart of the Apennines

The harsh climate, dark gorges and dense forests of the Marsica Mountains are, without doubt, the most characteristic features of the Abruzzo National Park. The solitary Godi Pass offers a spectacular panorama of the Meta mountains and the National Park in all its vastness. Encircled in a majestic ring of mountains, the green vegetation of the Park stretches out as far as the upper Valle del Sangro and the wild Devil's Pass. The National Park offers a wealth of paths and panoramic views, especially around the Camosciara and the enchanting Val Fondillo, famous for its magic Grotto delle Fate ('Fairies' Grotto').

454 The dark shape of a crow stands out in the light of the moon.

454-455 The chamois live in perfect harmony with the natural environment of the Abruzzo Park.

455 top *Moonlight gives a silvery glow to the peaks of the Marsica mountains.*

456 *A pair of deer hide in the shade of a clearing.*

457 It is not uncommon to meet the gentle gaze of a roe deer along the paths of the park.

Ancient rituals

Built on a ridge of Monte Luparo at a height of 2989 ft (906 m) stands the little village of Cocullo, a handful of small houses that fit perfectly in the deep green setting of the surrounding Abruzzo countryside. Here, every year on the first Thursday in May, in honour of St. Dominic, the Processione dei Serpari ('Procession of the Snake Catchers') is held. This spectacular religious ceremony, unique in the world for its curious tradition involving parading with live snakes coiled around the neck, originates from medieval rituals and ancient folk beliefs.

The highlight of the Easter festivities held in the town of Sulmona is the traditional 'Procession of the Madonna Rushing to the Square.' The whole town, joined by a great number of tourists, watch this lively event, which represents a heritage of local ancient customs. The heavy structure on which the Madonna stands is carried on the shoulders of members of an ancient confraternity. The origins of this ritual, which were perhaps Christianized in a later period, date back to the earliest Christian times.

Southern snows

The vast plateau of the Sila chain stretches out between the gulfs of Taranto and Squillace, with large expanses of woodland broken up by parallel chains of mountains. In the center the Sila Grande is the tallest and most popular of the chain. Monte Botte Donato 6270 ft (1900 m) and three artificial lakes animate the landscape and make this part of the Sila chain the largest water reservoir of Southern Italy. The vegetation is characterized by the Corsican pine, a subspecies of the Austrian black pine, which in Italy grows only in Calabria and Sicily. On the mountainsides, meanwhile, grow dense woodlands of beech.

462 Snow-covered forests and solitary plains characterize the uniquely beautiful natural landscape of the Sila mountains.

463 The plateau of the Sila chain is a paradise for cross-country skiers, offering a number of remarkable trails such as that which crosses from Monte Curcio to the slopes of Monte Botte Donato.

464-465 The strange shape of a group of Corsican pines completely covered with snow, near Monte Curcio, give the landscape a curious appearance.

466-467 The vast lakes scourged by the wind are a fundamental element of the Sila mountains.

228 and 229 The flight of the seagull admirably encompasses all the principles of aerodynamics.